A HISTORY *of the* Wheeler *Family*

SECOND EDITION

A HISTORY *of the* Wheeler *Family*

SECOND EDITION

Originally compiled August 1994

Revised February 2017

A HISTORY OF THE WHEELER FAMILY
Revised 2017

Copyright © 2017 by Bruce "Buzz" Wheeler
Prepared for publication by Stellar Communications Houston

This book is protected under the copyright laws of the United States of America. Any reproduction or other unauthorized use of the material herein is prohibited without the express written permission of the author. For information, contact Stellar Communications Houston.

The author has endeavored to recount and compile events, conversations, and data as accurately as possible.

Originally compiled by Lloyd Wheeler and William Wheeler, August 1994. Revised February 2017.

Published in the United States of America.

A History of the Wheeler Family

Hardcover ISBN 978-1-944952-19-8

Stellar Communications Houston
www.stellarwriter.com
281.804.7089

A LETTER *to the* FAMILY
1994

Dear Family,

When the idea of a Wheeler family reunion was first put forward in early 1993 we felt it would be an unusual event. Of course, in the 1960s and 1970s the Wheelers and Swansons would get together almost every Thanksgiving and Christmas at Ted and Margaret's home in Grand Island. But now the children, grandchildren and great grandchildren of Ted and Margaret live in ten different states with a majority residing outside of Nebraska. Family reunions are likely to be very special occasions from here on out. Mary Kay (Wheeler) Tuma deserves a lot of thanks for bringing all of us together.

Because of the special nature of this family reunion (and because we had plenty of warning) we decided to put together some type of document about the history of the Wheelers, and this book is the product of that effort. The question "Where did I come from?" is a popular topic in our society today. Many people can answer that question in part by pointing to some ethnic culture or tradition, but the Wheelers have been in North America so long that we can only guess about our European roots. Many of our family's traditions and beliefs have been formed out of the lives of our recent ancestors (including, and maybe especially, Ted and Margaret's lives). We're willing to wager that as you read this book you will recognize something about yourself. At the very least, when someone asks "Where did you come from?" you will be able to speak with some authority.

The information in this book comes from U.S. census records, history books, newspaper articles, photographs, questionnaires filled out by family members and memories. We have tried to be as factual as possible, but we cannot guarantee that everything in this book is accurate. We hope you enjoy reading this history. We certainly had fun putting it together.

Sincerely,
  Lloyd J. Wheeler & William J. Wheeler

A LETTER *to the* FAMILY
2017

Dear Family,

For the past 20+ years, I have treasured the original volume of Wheeler Family History written by my dad and Bill. But a lot has happened in the lives of us Wheelers since that original volume was published. I've enjoyed hearing of your lives and accomplishments through the years, and I decided that it was time to update this book with the happenings of the last two decades. Along the way, we've collected additional memories of days gone by, and we're pleased to add those in this volume as well.

I can't help but smile when I think of my hardworking grandparents taking a risk on that first Wheeler's store — what would they think if they could see how their legacy has impacted so many generations? We Wheelers are now scattered all over the country, living out our own versions of love and achievement.

But our family's success and mobility comes at a cost, which is the loss of our rich legacy of stories. Back in 1994, my dad and Bill did their part to preserve our family's history: compiling a book that chronicled Wheeler history in America up until that point. Over the past year, I asked for your help in updating their family history book with the happenings of the last few decades.

And you certainly came through! I think the book will be something we'll all enjoy, and it will allow us to share our stories with our children and grandchildren. Thanks for your help with the project.

Sincerely,
    Buzz Wheeler

How our fathers toiled and how much they suffered, we, their descendants, who are now enjoying the fruits of their labors, can never realize or know; we owe them a debt of gratitude which we can never pay. The best we can do, is to live worthy lives, and try to keep green the memories of those who did so little for themselves and so much for us.

From *The First Chapter of Norwegian Immigration*, by Rasmus B. Anderson, 1896

TABLE of CONTENTS

I. EARLY ANCESTORS 1
    The Wheelers 7
    The Clarks 9
    The Andersons 10
    The Greens 14
    The Cooks 15

II. WILLIAM A. & CATHERINE A. WHEELER 17

III. WILLIAM H. & SARAH P. WHEELER 33

IV. LLOYD H. & MARGARET M. WHEELER 53
    Early Years 59
    Farming 64
    Clarissa 67
    Battle Lake 87
    Nebraska 101
    Arizona 147

V. DESCENDANTS OF LLOYD H. & MARGARET M. WHEELER 161
    Lloyd J. Wheeler Family 163
    James H. Wheeler Family 189
    Shirley A. Eberspacher Family 213
    Beverly J. Swanson Family 249

INDEX 279

I. EARLY ANCESTORS

LLOYD H. WHEELER
Family Tree

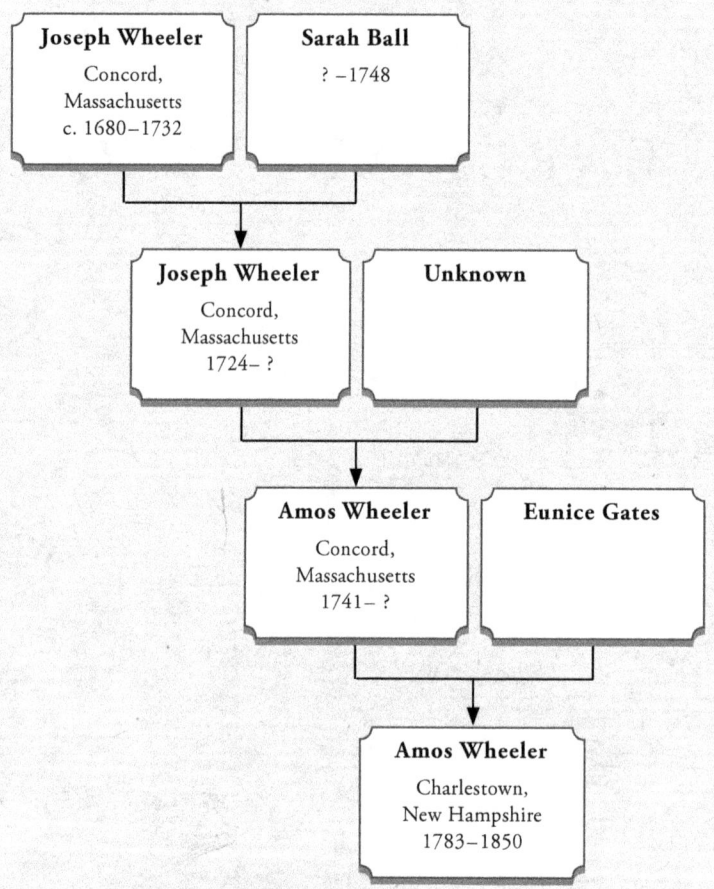

LLOYD H. WHEELER
Family Tree

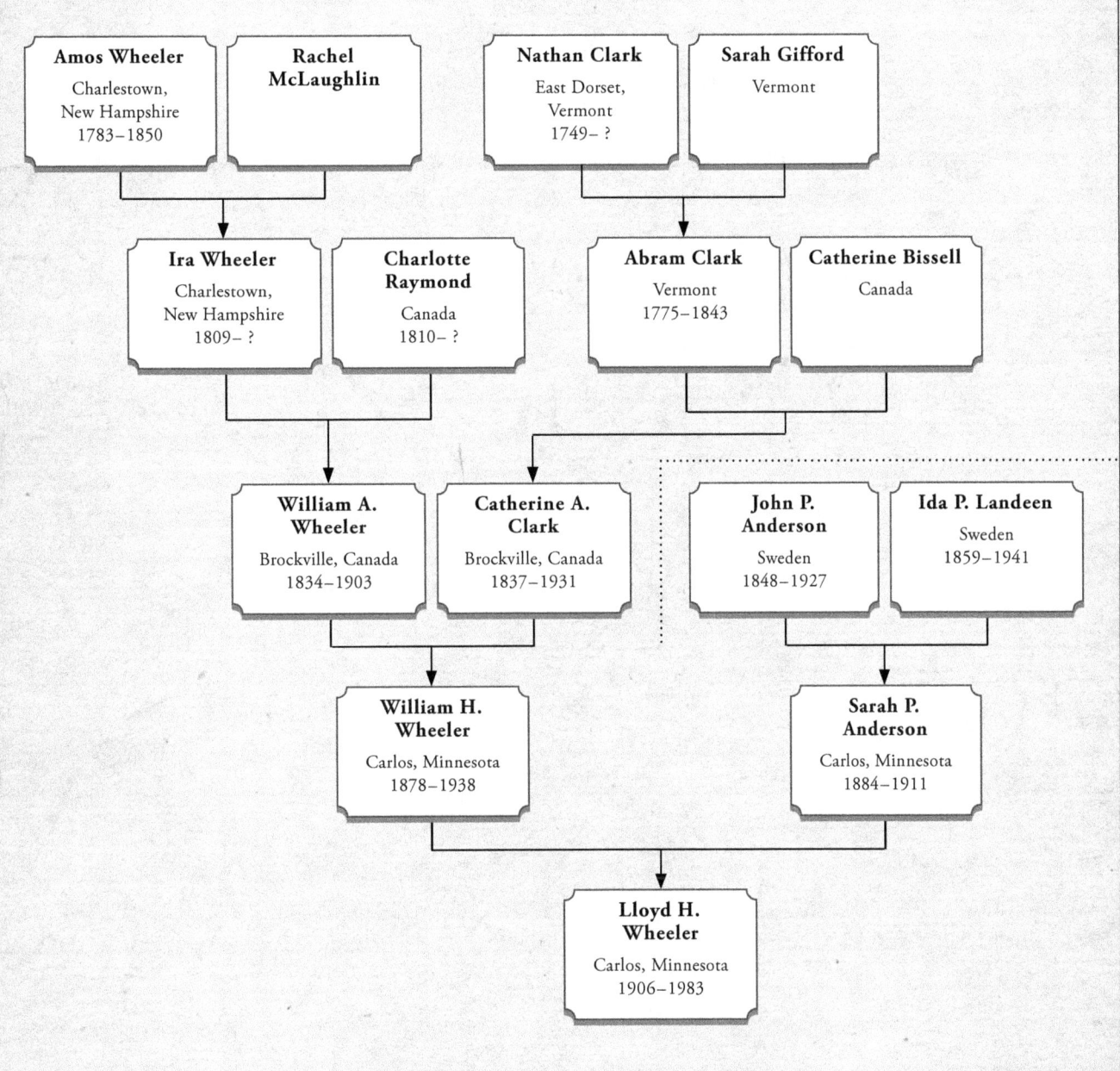

MARGARET M. GREEN
Family Tree

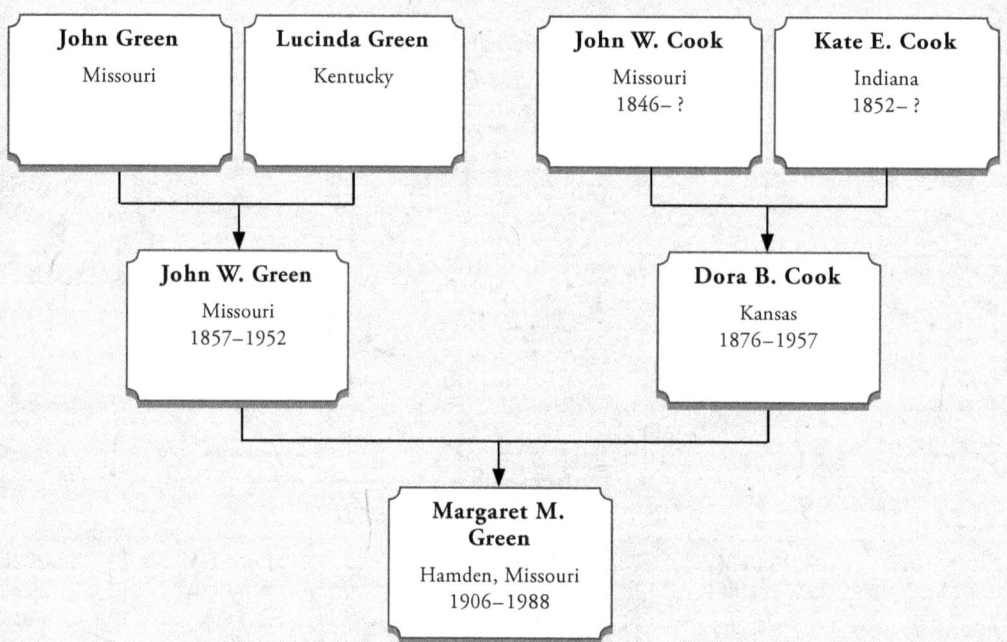

JOHN W. GREEN
Family Tree

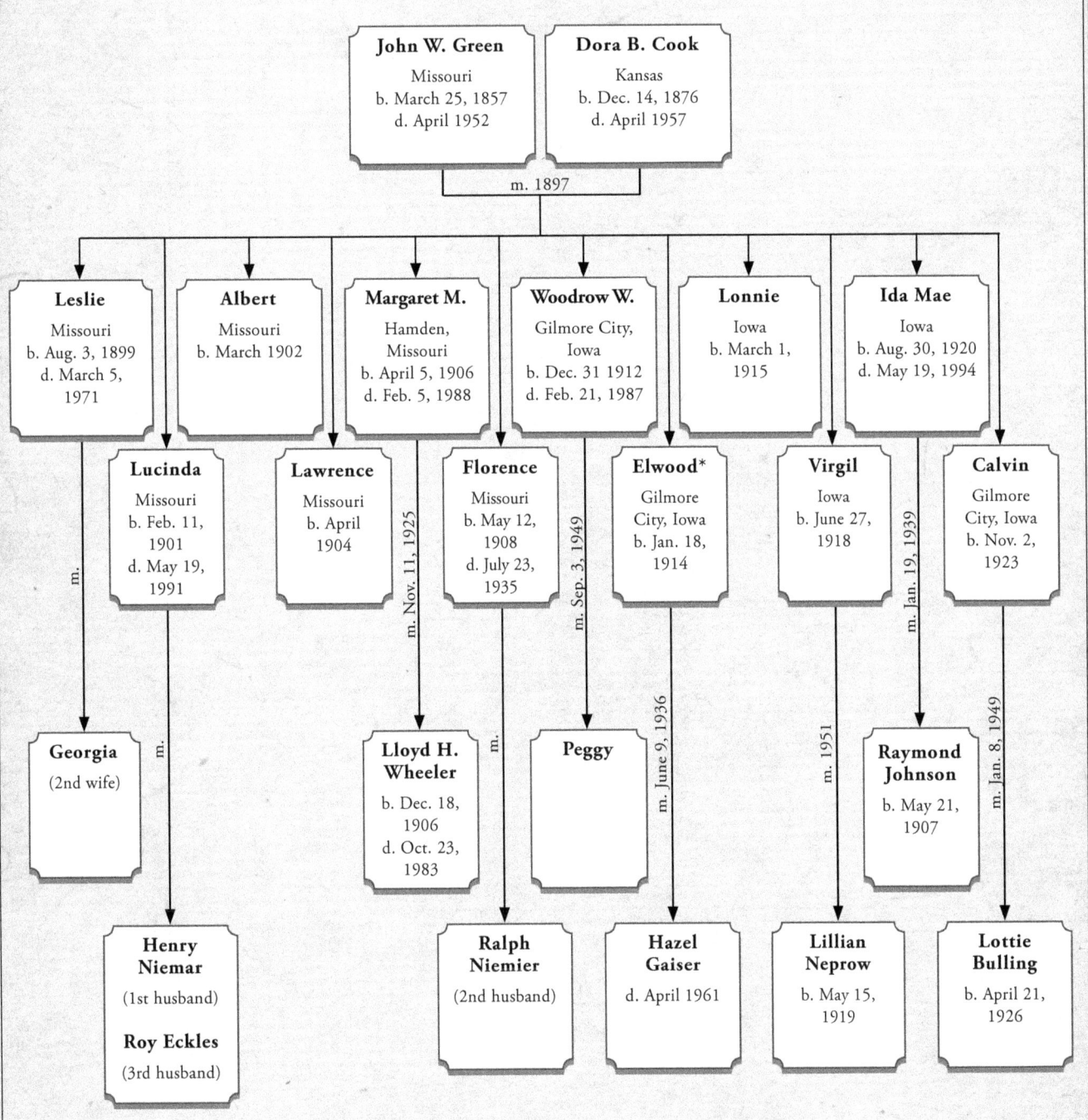

*Second wife is Marie Wagner, who was born August 25, 1927. They were married on December 7, 1962.

There are five distinct families which make up the known ancestors of Lloyd H. ("Ted") Wheeler and Margaret M. Green. Besides the Wheelers and the Greens, they include the Clarks, the Andersons, and the Cooks. The family trees shown on the previous pages identify the known ancestors and demonstrate their relationship to each other. What has been discovered about the early ancestors of these five families is described in greater detail below. With more time (and access to Canadian census records) it may be possible to learn more about each of these families.

THE WHEELERS

The Wheelers have, with certainty, been traced back to Ira Wheeler, who was probably born in Charlestown, New Hampshire, on June 15, 1809. A "History of Northern Minnesota" written in 1902 suggests that Ira was born in New York State but he is quite likely the Ira Wheeler born in New Hampshire who is identified in "The History of the Wheeler Family in America" written in 1914. If the latter book is correct then it is possible to trace the Wheelers back to a Joseph Wheeler who was born in Concord, Massachusetts, around 1680.

The Wheelers have been in America a long time. The history mentioned above claims that Wheeler was the most common name in America prior to 1650. There were Wheelers in Massachusetts, Connecticut, New York, Pennsylvania, Maryland, and Virginia: in Concord, Massachusetts, 35 families bore the name in 1640. These early Wheelers were Puritans and, like many others who emigrated to America during this period, they were fleeing from religious persecution in England. Many of the Wheelers apparently came from Odell, in the county of Bedford, in England.

Charlotte (Raymond) Wheeler, (1810 - ?)

The origin of the name Wheeler doesn't have anything to do with making wheels, e.g. a wheelwright. It's an old Saxon name, originally spelled Wielher, which first appeared in the eighth century when surnames were quite rare and were often not passed on from generation to generation. Wielher is the compound of two separate Anglo-Saxon words: "wiel" meaning prosperous or fortunate and "heri" meaning warrior or hero. So the modern translation of Wheeler might be "the lucky warrior" or "the prosperous hero."

Returning to Ira, he was a shoemaker, and sometime early in his life he moved to Canada, where he met and married Charlotte Raymond. Charlotte was born in Canada on January 19, 1810, and, although her date of death has not been discovered, she is known to have lived to at least age 93. Charlotte's father was born in Vermont and her mother was from Canada.

Ira and Charlotte had a son, William Amos Wheeler, who was born in Brockville, Ontario, Canada, on October 17, 1834. William went to public school, and, even though Ira died when he was quite young, William learned his father's trade. A short biography of William A. in the "History of Northern Minnesota" explains that being a shoemaker was not "suited to his tastes" so he "turned his attention to agriculture" and also "was handy with tools and learned the carpenter's trade." William A. Wheeler married Catherine A. Clark on February 14, 1859 (Valentine's Day). A description of the remainder of their lives is given later in this history.

William A. Wheeler (1834-1903) and Catherine A. (Clark) Wheeler (1837-1931)

Ira and Charlotte are believed to have had nine children, four of whom were still alive in 1900. Charlotte eventually followed some of her children, including William A., to the United States and Minnesota. According to U.S. Census records, in 1900 she was living in Hastings, Minnesota, with her daughter, Chloe Truax. Chloe, a dressmaker, was born in February, 1839 in Canada. She gave birth to six children, three of whom were alive in 1900. The census records also indicate that she was divorced. Chloe emigrated from Canada to the United States in 1857.

THE CLARKS

Catherine A. Clark's ancestors were described in a newspaper article found in Margaret Wheeler's Bible. The article, entitled "Fairfield and Its Pioneers," is from *The Recorder and Times*, April 11, 1927 of Fairfield East, Canada. The article describes the early pioneers of Fairfield and mentions Nathan Clark, who was born in East Dorset, Vermont, on June 16, 1749. Nathan married Sarah Gifford on March 23, 1775, and together they had seven children between 1775 and 1791. The eldest, Abram (sometimes called Hiram), was born in 1775 and later married Catherine Bissell, a Canadian. The 1790 U.S. Census shows the Clarks living in "Dorsett Township" of Bennington County. Umphory Gifford's family lived adjacent to the Clarks. This was probably Sarah's father or brother.

In March 1794, the Clarks left East Dorset, Vermont, and moved to Canada, becoming one of the early settlers of Fairfield a few years later. The article explains that the Clarks were part of a group known as the "United Empire Loyalists" who emigrated to Canada during this period:

> These people had previously lived, no doubt, happily, somewhere in America, or United States now, but who, preferring to suffer persecution, loss of property, as well as danger of losing their lives, remained true to their king, their flag, and their conscience. Consequently they found that residing in the States became unbearable (being looked upon as rebels, traitors and outlaws), so they separated themselves from home and friends to seek homes in primitive Upper Canada. On arrival here they found the land in the district of Johnstown, along the St. Lawrence river, a veritable wilderness, but undaunted they preferred to start anew, so secured land.

In 1821, Nathan Clark purchased 200 acres and a log cabin from Peter McEathron. There is a legend about the Clark farm that a pot of gold was buried somewhere on it during the War of 1812. "Many seekers and diggers came to search for the gold, but no one was ever successful in finding it." After Nathan Clark died, one of his sons, Robert, assumed ownership of the farm. The Clark family still lived on the farm as of 1927, the date of the article.

Little is known about Abram Clark (Nathan's oldest son) and Catherine Bissell. It may be that a generation has been skipped because when Catherine A. Clark was born on December 1,

1837, in Brockville, Ontario, Abram would have been 62 years old. Catherine's father may actually have been Hiram, possibly the son of Abram, but this confusion can only be solved by an examination of the Canadian census records. A sister of Catherine's, Lib Cole, is mentioned as still being alive in New York state when Catherine died in 1931. Although it could not be confirmed, it appears that other members of the Clark family joined Catherine and her husband in Minnesota. Abram died in 1843 at age 68.

Photo taken by Lois Wheeler in 1920 of Hiram Clark's farm home outside of Fairfield East, Canada

THE ANDERSONS

John P. Anderson and Ida P. Landeen were the last of the early ancestors to emigrate to the United States. John was born in Sweden on May 12, 1848, and came to Carlos, Minnesota in 1881 at the age of 33. Ida was born in Sweden on July 12, 1859, and arrived in the United States in 1882 at age 23. Ida had a brother, John V. Landeen (1861-1918), who later operated a saloon in Carlos. John and Ida were married in 1883, and when they went to Alexandria to get the marriage license, they rode on a sled filled with Christmas trees.

Their first child, Sarah Pauline Anderson, was born on September 22, 1884. Sarah married William H. Wheeler on June 25, 1904. A description of their lives is given later in this history. John and Ida had three other children, Helmer ("Ole"), Edith, and Frances, who were born between 1886 and 1894. John and Ida farmed outside of Carlos for many years. John died at the age of 79 on May 21, 1927, while Ida lived to age 81, dying on May 26, 1941.

In 1882, prior to her marriage to John Anderson, Ida gave birth to a daughter in Sweden named Helen. Helen also emigrated to Minnesota and later married George ("Mack") McCarn, who was originally from New York. Together they owned and operated the Hunters Hot Springs Hotel in Park County, Montana. The hotel was just north of Yellowstone National Park. Hunters Hot

Ida P. (Landeen) Anderson, (1859-1941)

Springs was famous for its hot and cold springs and mineral water, which were said to have a healing effect. George and Helen bought the hotel sometime in the early 1900s. Ida enjoyed Hunters Hot Springs and stayed out there often. Ole and his wife Nora also worked at the hotel in the late 1920s. Nora did the laundry, while one of Ole's jobs was to pick up guests at the train station every day at five o'clock. Ole would say that the guests came to the hotel on stretchers but would be walking when they left.

Later, Mack McCarn committed suicide and though the reason is not clear, alcoholism was suspected. Helen continued to operate the hotel for several years until it was destroyed by fire. She moved to Billings, Montana, and later died in 1948 in Colorado Springs, Colorado. Helen and Mack are reputed to be buried in Billings, but this has not been confirmed. Helen had a daughter, Dora, who was born out of wedlock in 1900. She died in 1910 and is buried in the Carlos cemetery. Helen also owned a travertine mine in Park County, Montana, the ownership of which, upon her death, transferred to her three living siblings and the three sons of Sarah.

Helen (Anderson) McCarn (1882-1948), Ida P. (Landeen) Anderson (1859-1941), and George ("Mack") McCarn

Hunters Hot Springs Hotel in Montana

The mine was successful and Lloyd H. ("Ted") Wheeler received between $5,000 and $10,000 in profits in the 1950s.

Helmer John ("Ole") Anderson was born on July 4, 1886. He married Nora E. Wheeler (one of Ira's daughters) on July 31, 1912. Ole and Nora farmed outside of Carlos and later worked at Hunters Hot Springs. Ole also operated a restaurant and beer tavern in Carlos. They had two children, both of whom were born in Carlos: Eugene ("Gene") John was born on May 25, 1913, and Leona L. ("Sis") was born on April 18, 1916. Ole died at age 88 on September 10, 1974, and Nora died at age 84 on February 20, 1977.

Some of the Anderson family in 1928: from left to right - Otto Gutzman, Edith (Anderson) Gutzman, Nora (Wheeler) Anderson, Helen (Anderson) McCarn, Ole Anderson, and Leona ("Sis") Anderson

Gene Anderson married Gertrude A. Tabbert in 1937 and they had two children: Jane M. (born February 14, 1940) and Conner E. (born April 25, 1944). They live in Alexandria and also own Francis (Anderson) Fenske's cabin on Lake Miltona. Sis Anderson married William K. Wicken in 1945 and they had one son: Allen W. (born July 7, 1946). They were divorced in 1954. Sis likes to garden, raising flowers and taking care of her lawn, and is active in her church. She also visits the residents of Alexandria's nursing homes, including Bert Wheeler, and always has a smile on her face.

Edith V. Anderson was born on May 3, 1890, and married Otto Gutzman in 1921. Otto was born in March 1875 and grew up on a farm near the William A. Wheeler farm. Edith and Otto lived on this farm for many years. Edith died at age 97 on March 5, 1988. Frances Anderson was born on May 3, 1894, and married Edward Otto Fenske in 1919. The 1920 U.S. Census showed Ed and Francis living with John and Ida Anderson on their farm. At that time Ed was a lineman for the telephone company, but he later owned a garage in Carlos. Whenever any of the younger Wheeler children were in Carlos, they would stop by Ed's garage and he would give them a nickel so they could buy candy or get an ice cream cone. Frances died at age 85 on March 8, 1980.

THE GREENS

John William Green was born in Missouri on March 25, 1857. His father, John Green, was born in Missouri, and his mother, whose name is believed to be Lucinda, was born in Kentucky, but little else is known about them. The Census records show that in 1900 John W. Green was living with his wife Dora Beatrice (Cook) Green and a newborn son, Leslie, on a farm in Musselfork Township, Chariton County, Missouri. Margaret, or "Maggie," John and Dora's fifth child, would be born six years later. Also living with the family in 1900 was Dora's father, John William Cook. The records indicate that he was a mailman.

Dora B. (Cook) Green (1876-1957) and John W. Green (1857-1952)

THE COOKS

John William Cook was born in November 1846 in Missouri. His father was born in either Kentucky or Missouri (there are conflicting records) and his mother was born in Missouri. The Census records indicate that in 1880 John W. Cook was living on a farm in Holt County, Missouri, with his wife, Kate E. Cook, and two children, William H. Cook, age six, and Dora, age four. Dora was born in Kansas on December 14, 1876. Kate E. Cook was born around 1852, probably in Indiana. Her parents were from Ohio. Little else is known about the Cooks.

II. WILLIAM A. & CATHERINE A. WHEELER

WILLIAM AMOS WHEELER
Family Tree

William A. Wheeler
Brockville, Canada
b. Oct. 17, 1834
d. Jan. 15, 1903

Catherine A. Clark
Brockville, Canada
b. Dec. 1, 1837
d. Dec. 7, 1931

m. February 14, 1859

Mary A.
Canada
b. Jan. 8, 1860
d. Sep. 5, 1910

Ira H.
Canada
b. Oct. 28, 1863
d. March 5, 1941

Eva
Carlos, Minnesota
b. 1870

Charlotte
Carlos, Minnesota
b. Nov. 3, 1874

William Henry
Carlos, Minnesota
b. Aug. 14, 1878
d. Dec. 24, 1938

Lois E.
Carlos, Minnesota
b. Nov. 1882
d. 1968

m. 1883

Emma F.
Canada
b. 1861
d. 1910

m. 1892

Edgar
Hastings, Minnesota
b. 1867

Wilson
Carlos, Minnesota
b. Feb. 20, 1872
d. March 4, 1873

Stephen C.
Carlos, Minnesota
b. 1876
d. 1915

m. June 25, 1904

Katherine J.
Carlos, Minnesota
b. Oct. 1880
d. 1934

m.

Terrence H. Weatherhead
b. April 16, 1861

Oliver Hartman

Lena L. Engfer
b. Oct. 30, 1870
d. Dec. 18, 1935

Gustave Lund

Albert Darch

Sarah P. Anderson
b. Sep. 22, 1884
d. Oct. 16, 1911

Frank Sweet
b. 1881
d. 1923

Mattie 1884 - ?
Josie 1886 - 1903
Cleveland 1888 - ?
Robert 1890 - 1960
Hazel B. 1892 - ?
Bessie E. 1901 - ?

Nora E. 1892 - 1977
Charles S. 1894 - 1967
William J. 1896 - 1964
Charlotte 1897 - 1985
Paul 1899 - 1977
Minnie 1901 - ?
Angus I. 1902 - 1975
Louis 1905 - 1967
Floyd E. 1907 - ?
Bertram 1909 - ?
Otis 1912 - ?

Howard O. 1905 - 1984
Lloyd H. 1906 - 1983
Leslie E. 1909 - 1973
*Dorothy E. 1922 - ?

* Mother is Bertha Jacobs, William H. Wheeler's second wife. m. 1920.

IRA H. WHEELER
Family Tree

Ira H. Wheeler
Canada
b. Oct. 28, 1863
d. March 5, 1941

Lena L. Engfer
Belle Plaine, Minnesota
b. Oct. 30, 1870
d. Dec. 18, 1935

m. July 22, 1892

Nora E. 1892 - 1977 — m. 1912 — **Helmer J. Anderson**
- Eugene J. 1913 - 2002
- Leona L. 1916 - 1995

William J. 1896 - 1964 — m. — **Charles S.** 1894 - 1967 / **Edna Klug** (m. 1922)
- DeEtte
- Yvonne
- Lanea
- Charlene
- Bertram 1943 -

Charles S. 1894 - 1967 — **Katie Stark**

Charlotte 1897 - 1985 — m. 1919 — **Clarence Landeen**
- Glen C. 1921 - 2010
- Gladys 1925 - 2013
- Florence
- Marie
- Howard 1940 -

Arlette 1921 -
Marvin 1922 - 1989

Paul 1899 - 1977 — m. — **Esther Johnson** — **Anton Brakken**
- Phyllis E. 1929 -
- Dolores I. 1930 -
- Delbert E. 1935 -

Norman 1922 - 2015
Betty 1926 -

Angus I. 1902 - 1975 — m. — **Minnie** 1901 -

Louis F. 1905 - 1967 — m. 1923 — **Mary E. Stark** — **Francis Andrews**
- Robert M. 1923 - 1982
- Lester A. 1925 -
- Eunice M. 1927 -
- Donna M. 1932 -
- Mary Ann 1939 -
- *David L. 1949 -
- *John R. 1951 -
- *Sharon S. 1952 -
- *Keith D. 1955 -
- *Robin J. 1959 -
- *Jeffrey A. 1965 -
- *Gregory E. 1967 -
- *Michael S. 1968 -
- *Steven M. 1969 -

Floyd E. 1907 - 2002 — m. 1932 — **Bertram** 1909 - 1996 — **Mildred I. Nelson** — **Cordelia Enright**
- Donald 1932 - 1966
- Dale K. 1938 -

Charles I. 1931 - 1971
Lova 1933 -
Mona 1935 -
Wallace F. 1935 -

Otis 1912 - — m. — **Adeline Hink**
- Janet 1939 -
- JoAnn
- Judy

*Mother is Gloria J. Pascol, second wife of Angus I. Wheeler

II. WILLIAM A. & CATHERINE A. WHEELER

William and Catherine were married in Canada on Valentine's Day, February 14, 1859. They had three children while living in Canada: Mary A. was born on January 8, 1860, Emma F. in 1861, and Ira H. on October 28, 1863. The Wheelers left Canada in 1863 and lived somewhere in New York State for two years. They then moved to Mercer County, Pennsylvania, in 1865 where William worked on the Jamestown & Franklin Railroad for one year. The family then moved to Hastings, which is on the Mississippi River, in Dakota County, Minnesota, in 1866 where William worked on a farm. They probably went to Hastings because of either relatives or friends who already lived there. In 1867, another son, Edgar, was born. The family then moved to Douglas County, Minnesota, in January 1868, homesteading 160 acres in Section II of Carlos Township. The Wheelers would remain on this farm for the next 70 years.

In 1868, Douglas County could be described as the frontier. The first settlers came to Douglas County in 1858, the same year that Minnesota was admitted into the Union as a state. The Red River trail passed through the county, connecting the Mississippi River and the Red River (which forms the border between Minnesota and North Dakota). The 1860 U.S. Census listed 71 men in the county, 35 of which were married, and 78 children. In August

William A. Wheeler (1834-1903)

Catherine A. (Clark) Wheeler (1837-1931)

1862 the great Sioux uprising broke out in Minnesota, one of the most savage Indian-settler conflicts in history, and many settlers fled until a government post with a squad of soldiers was set up in Alexandria. The first settlers were "Yankees" from the New England states, but following the end of the Civil War in 1865 a wave of immigrants from Northern Europe came to the area to find homesteads. The railroad line ended in St. Cloud, Minnesota, after which settlers walked or rode stages or wagons the remaining 60 miles to Douglas County. In 1878, the railroad was finished to Alexandria and the influx of settlers increased.

Douglas County is an excellent example of why Minnesota is called "the land of 10,000 lakes." The county contains 723 square miles, of which approximately one-seventh is water, with 264 named lakes. As it was 100 years ago, the county is still quite rural, with the economy based mainly on agriculture. In 1910, the population of Douglas County was almost 18,000. In 1990, eighty years later, the population had increased to 30,000.

The Wheelers homesteaded on a farm that is about two and one-half miles from Carlos, though the town of Carlos didn't exist at the time. The farm is also approximately 10 miles north of Alexandria on Highway 29. At first the family lived in a tent. William then built a two room shanty of hewed logs with a trough roof which served as their home until 1876. The log cabin must have had windows because Catherine would later recall that Indians sometimes peered through them. Indians still lived along the Long Prairie River, which runs next to Carlos. The Indians often traded venison or bear meat for rutabagas, potatoes or bread from the settlers. The 1870 U.S. Census taker found a family of seven Wheelers living in this log cabin. William was 35; Catherine was 32; Mary, their eldest daughter, was 10; Emma was eight; Ira was seven; Edgar was three; and there was a new baby, Eva. The Census taker valued the family's real estate at $230 and their personal property at $100.

The next few years saw William and Catherine continuing to prosper and expand their family. Besides clearing and farming the land, William was a carpenter and assisted in erecting many buildings in Alexandria. Catherine gave birth to six more children over the next 12 years. Wilson Wheeler was born on February 20, 1872, but then died from Scarlet fever on March 4, 1873. Charlotte Wheeler was born on November 3, 1874; Stephen C. Wheeler was born in 1876; William H. Wheeler was born on August 14, 1878; Katherine J. Wheeler was born in October of 1880; and Lois E. Wheeler was born in November 1882. A new house was built in 1875 and described as "a commodious farm residence better suited to the times."

This was the new house as photographed in 1912. Catherine A. (Clark) Wheeler is on the right, her son William H. Wheeler is to the left, and his three sons (Howard, Ted and Les) are between them.

William and Catherine's children began to grow up and move away from home. In 1882, Ira homesteaded next to his father at the age 19. He married Lena L. Engfer in 1892, and together they had 11 children.

Mary married Terrence Henry Weatherhead in 1883 and together they had six children. Terry and Mary lived in several different locations in the area, including a farm which was on a stage route between Alexandria and Parkers Prairie. The Weatherheads were on the first telephone line between the two towns. They eventually moved to Alexandria in 1905, where Terry began the Weatherhead Ice Dray Line. Ice was cut on Lakes Henry, Agnes, and Latoka and then stored in a building in Alexandria. The ice was used in ice boxes, among other things, and was supposed to last all year until the following winter.

Mary died on September 5, 1910, at the age of 50. Emma married Oliver Hartman and moved to Fargo, North Dakota. She died in 1910 at the age of 49. Eva married Gustave Lund and moved to Fargo, North Dakota, then Utah, and later, Maywood, California. Charlotte ("Lottie") married Albert Darch, a popular railroad man, in Fargo.

In the 1880s and 1890s, William A. Wheeler assumed a public role in many of the

Ira H. Wheeler (1863-1941)

Lena L. (Engfer) Wheeler (1870-1935)

Ira and Lena Wheeler's children at Ira's funeral in 1941. From left to right: Nora (Wheeler) Anderson, Charles Wheeler, William Wheeler, Charlotte (Wheeler) Landeen, Paul Wheeler, Minnie (Wheeler) Brakken, Angus Wheeler, Louis Wheeler, Floyd Wheeler, Bertram Wheeler, and Otis Wheeler

developments in the Carlos area. He served as justice of the peace and assessor in Carlos for a number of years. In March 1884, William led the effort to build the first schoolhouse in Carlos, District No. 69. Many of his children and grandchildren attended school there. The school was finally replaced in 1953 but still stands on the Douglas County Fairgrounds. William's obituary mentions his "conversion" in the 1880s. William helped found the Bethanay Lutheran Church in Carlos, which later merged with the Trinity Lutheran Church. William also led the effort to build the Carlos Union Church in 1900. An interesting agreement existed among the churches in Carlos at that time. Only the Union Church could conduct services in English; the St. Michael's German Church used German; and in the Scandinavian Church Swedish was spoken. The Union Church was destroyed by lightning on July 17, 1908. The altar was saved and is now at the Trinity Church in Carlos.

The schoolhouse for District No. 69 in Carlos was used from 1884 to 1953.

William A. Wheeler died on January 15, 1903, at the age of 68 from Bright's Disease and heart failure. His obituaries described a man who had lived a long and successful life:

"Mr. Wheeler undertook the making of a home in the then wilderness in his usual vigorous manner. He lived on the farm for thirty-six years and saw Carlos and the county bloom from a wilderness to a veritable garden. Mr. Wheeler was not only one of the old settlers of Carlos, he was one of the best respected, and justly so. The best of neighbors, always a worker for the best interests of his community, loyal to himself, his family, his neighbors. He will be more missed from the Carlos circle than perhaps almost any other man in that town."

A reporter for the Alexandria paper wrote that "thirty-two teams followed the remains from the house, showing the estimation in which the deceased was held in the community in which he has lived for so many years." William left his wife Catherine and 10 children. There were still four children living at home, including Stephen, age 26; Will, age 24; Kate, age 22; and Lois, age 20.

Catherine continued to live on the farm with her family. William H. Wheeler eventually took over the farm and in 1910, Catherine, age 72, lived with his family. In 1926, she moved to Alexandria and lived with her daughter Lois. Catherine died on December 7, 1931, at Lois' apartment in Alexandria at the age of 94. Her obituary described Catherine as "a woman of remarkable vitality and up until a few months ago was active in her home. Mrs. Wheeler was truly a pioneer woman and endured all the hardships of the early settler. She was a good Christian, devoted to her home and family and a loyal friend."

William A. Wheeler (1834 - 1903)   *Catherine A. (Clark) Wheeler (1837 - 1931)*

OLD SETTLERS PASS AWAY

William A. Wheeler of Carlos Dies After a Short Illness - Came to Carlos in 1867

W.A. WHEELER of Carlos, after a short illness, died last Friday at his home in that town.

Mr. Wheeler was one of the oldest settlers of the town of Carlos. He was born in Canada in November 1834, consequently was 68 years old last November. He was married in Canada and came to the United States in 1863 and was in Pennsylvania for a short time when he came to Hastings in this state and in 1867 with his family to Douglas county. He took the homestead in Carlos that has since been his home and moved with his wife and young children to the new home. Settlers there at that time were far between and the family underwent all the hardships of a new country. Mr. Wheeler was then in his young manhood and undertook the making of a home in the then wilderness in his usual vigorous manner. He lived on the farm for thirty-six years and saw Carlos and the county bloom from a wilderness to a veritable garden.

Mr. Wheeler was not only one of the old settlers of Carlos, he was one of the best respected, and justly so. The best of neighbors, always a worker for the best interests of his community, loyal to himself, his family, his neighbors. He will be more missed from the Carlos circle than perhaps almost any other man in that town. To his family and the church work in Carlos, his loss will be almost irreparable.

The deceased leaves besides a widow, ten children to mourn his loss. They are Mrs. T. H. Weatherhead of this village, Ira Wheeler, who owns a farm in Carlos, Edward, Stephen and Will, the two latter making their home with their parents; Mrs. Lottie Darch and Mrs. Emma Lund who live at Fargo, Miss Eva who has been in Utah and who came home for the funeral and Misses Kate and Lois who are at home.

The funeral occurred on Tuesday, the Rev. A. A. Thom officiating. Services were held at the home at one o'clock and at the Carlos Union church at two, the burial taking place in Carlos Union cemetery.

The family have the deep sympathy of many friends.

William A. Wheeler's obituary

DEATH OF AN OLD SETTLER

The town of Carlos mourns the loss of William A. Wheeler, one of its oldest settlers, who died on Thursday, Jan. 15, of bright's disease and heart failure.

The subject of our sketch was born in the province of Ontario, Canada, Oct. 17th, 1834. In 1859 he was married to Miss Catherine Clark, of Brockville, Ont., and in 1965 removed to Hastings in this state. Coming to Douglas county in 1868. Mr. and Mrs. Wheeler took a homestead in Carlos, where they have resided ever since. Previous to settling on his farm Mr. Wheeler worked as a carpenter, and assisted in erecting many of the buildings in this town, one of them being the old M. E. parsonage.

Four sons and six daughters survive the loss of one of the best fathers in Douglas County, viz: Ira, Ed, Steve and Will, Mrs. Terrence Weatherhead of Alexandria, Mrs. Hartman of Fargo and Misses Kate and Lois who live at the old home. All were present at the funeral with the exception of Mrs. Weatherhead, who was unable to be present because of illness in the family. Mr. Wheeler's mother also survives. She has reached the age of 93 and resides in the town of Hastings. The funeral was held at the Carlos Union church and burial was made in the adjoining cemetery. Thirty-two teams followed the remains from the house, showing the estimation in which the deceased was held in the community in which he lived for so many years. The service was conducted by the pastor, Rev. A. A. Thom, who spoke to the crowded assembly from John 9-4. "I must work the works of Him that sent me while it is called today." Miss Bundy officiated at the organ with her usual ability, being assisted by a special choir. The pall bearers were Messrs. H.F. Miller, Parnell Atkinson, A. Gutzman, J. Kohlhaas, Conrad Meister and Matt Yunt. The arrangements were under the direction of Mr. A. L. Sweet, whose services were simply invaluable. Indeed the writer has never seen a place in which funerals are conducted with greater ability than in Carlos township.

Mr. Wheeler was a devoted husband, an indulgent father and a firm friend and especially since his conversion, some fifteen years ago, has his influence always been for righteousness in the community. The erection of the Union church three years ago was largely due to his efforts and one of the last missions of his industrious life was to walk around the neighborhood soliciting subscriptions towards clearing this edifice from debt. This desired consummation he had the pleasure of seeing accomplished on Saturday January 3rd, less than two weeks before his death.

To his surviving widow and family will be accorded the spontaneous sympathy of all those who have known William A. Wheeler.

Mrs. Wheeler and family wish to express their heartfelt thanks to their many friends for kindest services rendered in connection with their one bereavement.

William A. Wheeler's obituary

MRS. CATHERINE WHEELER AGED NINETY-FOUR YEARS, DIES MONDAY MORNING

Mrs. Catherine Wheeler, aged ninety-four years, one of Alexandria's oldest residents, peacefully passed to her reward at her home Monday morning, at 2:35 o'clock. Infirmities, due to advanced age, were the cause of death.

She was a woman of remarkable vitality and up until a few months ago, was active in her home. Her decline the last few weeks was very marked and her passing, although not wholly unexpected, was a severe shock to her family.

Catherine Clark was born at Brockville, Ontario, Canada, December 1, 1837, and on Tuesday of last week, had reached her ninety-fourth birthday anniversary.

She lived in Canada about twenty-two years, when she was united in marriage with W.A. Wheeler, on February 14, 1959. After their marriage they moved to New York state, where they resided about two years. Then they moved to Hastings and lived there one year, after which they moved to Douglas county and settled on a farm in Carlos, where she has ever since resided, with the exception of the last five years that she has made her home with her daughter, Lois, in this city.

Mr. and Mrs. Wheeler were the parents of twelve children, one son and one daughter having died in infancy. Another son, Stephen died about sixteen years ago. Two daughters, Mary (Mrs. T. H. Weatherhead), passed away here in 1909, and Emma (Mrs. Oliver Hartman), died in 1910. Mr. Wheeler preceded his wife in death January 15, 1903.

The surviving children are: Ira H., and Wm. H. Wheeler of Carlos; Miss Lois, who lived at home; Eva (Mrs. G. A. Lund), Maywood, Cal.; Edgar Wheeler, Lottie (Mrs. Albert Darch), Catherine (Mrs. Frank Sweet), Fargo. There are thirty-seven grandchildren, fifty great grandchildren and one great great grandchild. One sister, Mrs. Cole of New York state, also survives.

Mrs. Wheeler was truly a pioneer woman and endured all the hardships of the early settler. She was a good Christian, devoted to her home and family and a loyal friend.

Funeral services were held Wednesday afternoon at 2:00 o'clock at Anderson's Funeral Home and at 2:15 from the Methodist church with Rev. J. R. Davies officiating.

A mixed quartet, consisting of Mr. and Mrs. E. E. Bauman, Mrs. Richard Chase and David Anderson, sang "Oh, for a Thousand Tongues to Tell," "Oh Love That Will Not Let Me Go" and "Have Thine Own Way." Mrs. Hugh Brown was accompanist.

Interment was made in the Carlos cemetery beside other members of the family. The pall bearers were: Nick Steidl, Mike Steidl, Isaac Atkinson, A. M. Kohlhaas, Peter Streed and Otto Gutzmann.

Friends of Grandma Wheeler were grieved to learn of her death at her home in Alexandria Monday morning. Sincere sympathy is extended to the bereaved family.

Catherine A. (Clark) Wheeler's obituary

III. WILLIAM H. & SARAH P. WHEELER

WILLIAM H. WHEELER
Family Tree

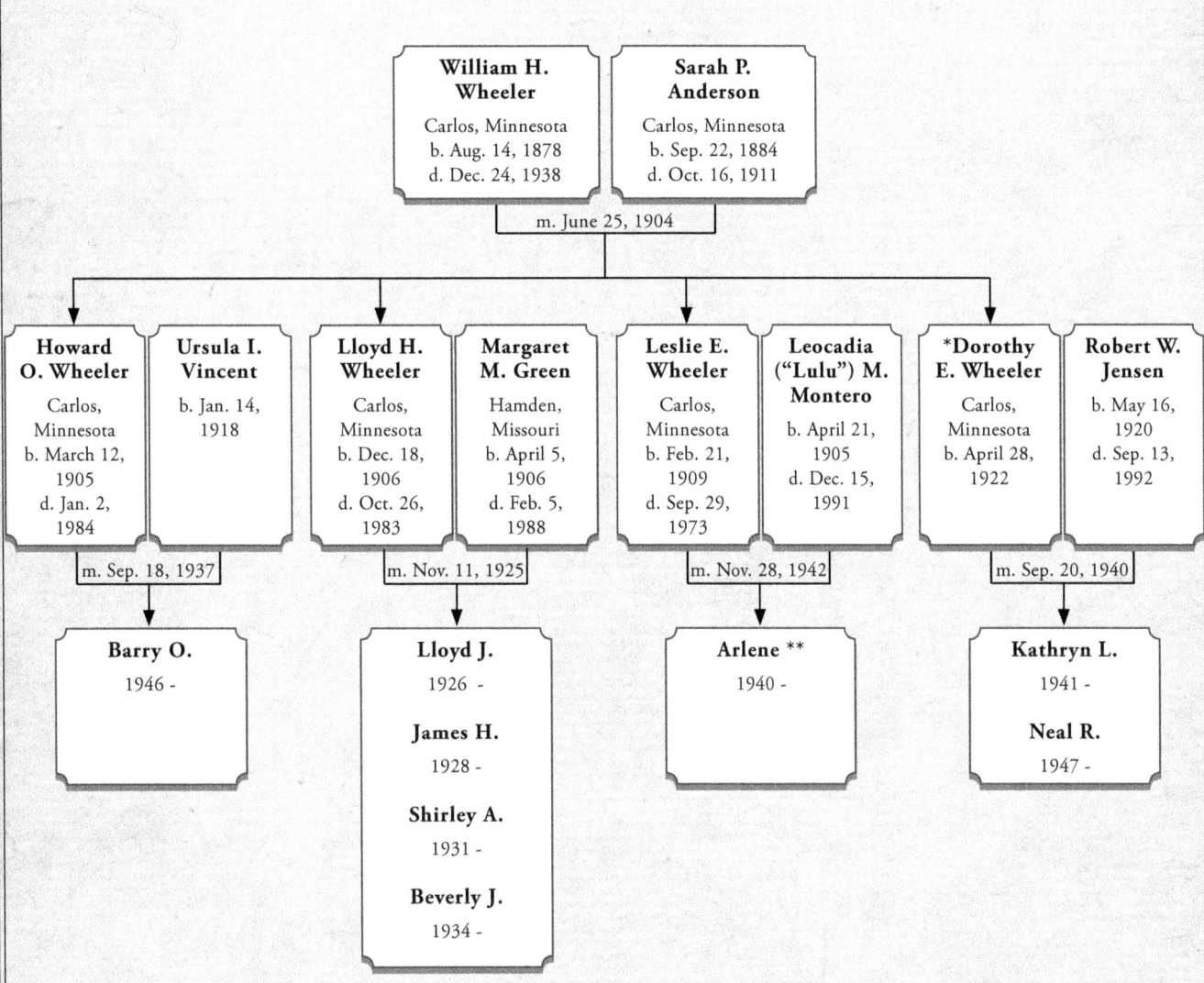

*Dorothy's mother was Bertha Louise Jacobs, William H. Wheeler's second wife. m. 1921.
** Arlene was adopted. She was Leocadia's granddaughter from an earlier marriage.

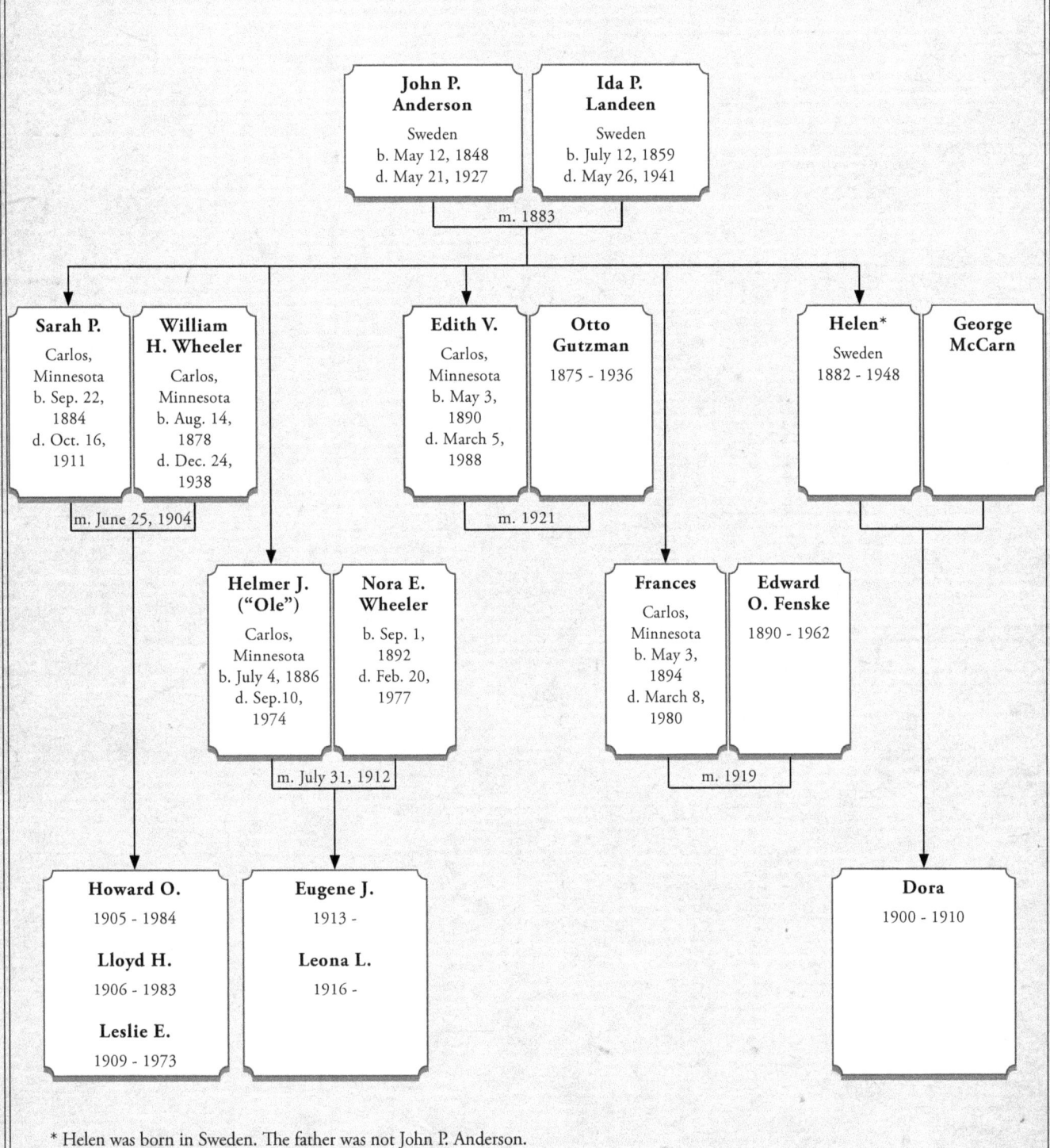

III. WILLIAM H. & SARAH P. WHEELER

William Henry Wheeler was born on August 14, 1878, at his parents' farm home in Carlos. He was the youngest son and the eighth child of 10 (who lived to adulthood). He attended District No. 69, the school his father had helped build, beginning in 1885 at age six. Hannah Fredenberg was his first teacher. When William H.'s father died in 1903, he was 24 and still living at home.

Sarah Pauline Anderson was born on September 22, 1884, in Carlos. Her parents had emigrated to Minnesota from Sweden only a few years earlier and so Sarah probably could speak Swedish as well as English. Sarah was the oldest of four children. She also attended District No. 69, the same school as William H., beginning in 1891 when she was six years old. In 1900, she was living with her parents and her sisters and brother on their farm outside Carlos.

William H. Wheeler (1878-1938)

On the right is Sarah P. (Anderson) Wheeler (1884-1911). The woman on the left is unknown.

Lloyd H. ("Ted") Wheeler, age 3

On June 25, 1904, William H. (age 25) and Sarah (age 19) were married. They almost certainly had known each other since they were young children. Sarah moved to the Wheeler farm and they immediately began a family. Howard O. was born on March 12, 1905, Lloyd H. ("Ted") was born on December 18, 1906, and Leslie E. was born on February 21, 1909.

By 1910, all of Will's siblings had left the farm. He lived there with Sarah, his three young sons, and his mother Catherine. Like his father, Will was a good carpenter. He built a barn in 1911 and a two story house in 1916. The house had an open stairway with a banister that children could slide down. Both the barn and the farmhouse are still in use today.

Barn on William H. Wheeler farm, built in 1911

Rear of William H. Wheeler farmhouse, built in 1916

Sarah died unexpectedly on October 16, 1911, while giving birth to a fourth child, who also died. However, her obituary mentions a "short illness of only nine days." She was 27 years old. Will was 33 and their three sons were ages six, four, and two. After Sarah died, Lois Wheeler, Will's sister, moved in to help raise the three boys.

Lois Wheeler is remembered fondly by several generations of Wheelers. She never married, but acted as a mother to Howard, Ted, and Les and as a grandmother to Ted's children. Margaret Wheeler wrote, "What a wonderful person. She (Lois) was like a mother to me." Jim Wheeler mentioned that "she came and stayed with us when mother (Margaret) was sick" and Bev Swanson said that Lois "had a way of making you feel special." In 1904, Lois, who was then 22, worked as a schoolteacher at District No. 69, the school her father had helped build. She was paid $35 a month, or $280 for the entire school year. Over the next several years she worked as a teacher in other schools in the area and eventually moved to Colorado. After raising Will's three boys, she moved to Alexandria and lived on the third floor of the Birchwood Apartments, working as a nurse for Dr. Haskell. Several people remembered having Christmas dinner at Lois' apartment, where she served oyster stew. Catherine, her mother, moved to Lois' apartment in the late 1920s, where Lois cared for her until she died in 1931. Lois died at age 86 in 1968.

DEATH OF MRS. WHEELER

Mrs. Sarah Wheeler, daughter of Mr. and Mrs. John Anderson and wife of Mr. Wm. Wheeler, died at her home in Carlos, Monday, Oct. 16th, after the short illness of nine days. On Sunday her condition was pronounced favorable and all were looking forward for her recovery, but she took a sudden change Monday and realizing that the death angel stood near, at 5 o'clock p.m., she called for all the relatives, saying she could not be with them longer and kissed them all good bye.

"Good Bye," but not forever,

Till we meet in the realms above.

Besides her loving husband and three small children, she leaves a father and mother, three sisters and one brother to mourn her loss. She was twenty-seven years of age. She was born and raised in Carlos and was of a friendly and lovable disposition. Seven years ago she was united in marriage with Wm. Wheeler of this place. Since then three children came to bless their home. On her death bed she asked her sister, Edith, to care for the little ones when she had gone, and she readily gave her consent to do so. Her funeral services were conducted by Rev. Benson, from the Swedish Lutheran church at this place, of which the deceased was a member. Her loss is felt throughout the community. It is indeed sad to have one so young and fair taken from our midst.

But he who knoweth best

Doeth all things well.

The funeral which was held Thursday, was largely attended. Among those from abroad were: Mrs. George McCarn of Livingston, Montana, a sister of Mrs. Wheeler; and Miss Lois Wheeler of Grand Junction, Colorado, sister of Mr. Wheeler, who will remain for a time and assist in caring for the bereaved family.

CARD OF THANKS.

We wish to extend our sincere and heartfelt gratitude to all who so kindly assisted us in our late bereavement, and also thank you for the many floral offerings.

WM. WHEELER, MR. AND MRS. JOHN ANDERSON AND FAMILY

Darling Sarah, we have loved thee
And thy loss we deeply feel.
But again we hope to meet thee
When life's trials all are o'er.
When our sorrows here are ended,
Then in Heaven with thee we'll dwell;
For 'tis God who has bereft us,
And in Him our souls we trust.
Jesus, while our hearts are bleeding
O'er the spoils that death has won,
We would at this solemn parting
Calmly say, Thy will be done;
Thou did'st give
And thou hast taken
Blessed Lord, Thy will be done.
Carlos, Minn.

Sarah P. (Anderson) Wheeler's obituary

From left to right: William H. Wheeler, the Palmers, and Lois Wheeler

William H. Wheeler with his three boys: Ted, Les, and Howard

After Sarah's death, Will and the family continued on the farm. Around 1920, Will placed an ad for a housekeeper and eventually hired Bertha Louise Jacobs. Bertha was born in Germany and had emigrated to the United States with her family when she was three years old. She later married and was widowed in 1918 when her first husband (named Hublou) and two of her children died during a flu epidemic in North Dakota. Four other children survived: Francis, George, Esther, and Evelyn. The relationship between Will and Bertha became romantic and they were married on November 15, 1920.

Will and Bertha then had a daughter, Dorothy Elizabeth, who was born on April 28, 1922. Dorothy grew up on the Wheeler farm outside of Carlos, attended District No. 69, and later graduated from Central High School in Alexandria in 1939. She married her high school sweetheart, Robert William Jensen, on September 20, 1940, and together they had two children: Kathryn Lorraine (born June 17, 1941) and Neal Robert (born November 5, 1947). Robert served in the Army in both World War II and the Korean War. They also operated a sheet metal business in Alexandria until retirement in 1970. Later, Dorothy and Robert began spending their winters in Lake Havasu City, Arizona, while retaining their home in Alexandria. Robert died on September 13, 1992, but Dorothy has continued to split her time between Alexandria and Arizona. Dorothy's sister Evelyn lives in Minneapolis and the two see each other often.

Dorothy E. (Wheeler) Jensen

In the 1920s, each of Will's sons moved away, while Will and Bertha continued to work on the farm raising corn and selling eggs for five cents a dozen. Howard went to Minneapolis where he worked for the railroad. He then lived in Iowa for a while and later moved to Michigan in 1935, joining several of Ira's sons, to work for General Motors. Ted left in 1924 at age 17 for Sioux City, Iowa, to look for work. Les joined the Navy in 1925 with his cousins, Bert and Floyd Wheeler, who were also sons of Ira Wheeler.

When Howard came to Michigan in 1935, he first worked in a General Motors plant in Grand Rapids, but later transferred to a plant in Pontiac.

A gathering of family and neighbors around 1925: from left to right – Esther Hublou, Ella Sikes (cousin), Leslie Wheeler, Ethel Sikes (cousin), George Hublou, (the next 3 people – child, woman with glasses, man with cap – are unknown), Bertha (Jacobs) Wheeler, (child in front of Bertha is unknown), William H. Wheeler, Dennis Christy (neighbor), Catherine A. (Clark) Wheeler, Dorothy Wheeler, Otis Christy (neighbor), Evelyn Hublou, Pauline Sikes (sister of Bertha), (the 2 children in front of her are unknown), Grandpa Jacobs (Bertha's father), Ralph Christy (neighbor) and Inger Christy (neighbor). Inger Christy was the midwife who helped in the delivery of Ted and Margaret Wheeler's children.

While in Pontiac, he lived with Angus Wheeler's family (one of Ira's sons) and often stopped at an Italian grocery in the neighborhood. In early 1937, Howard bought a new Oldsmobile and on February 16 (two days after Valentine's Day), he asked one of the girls who worked in the Italian grocery if she'd like to go out on a date in his new car. The girl's name was Ursula I. Vincent and she and Howard married on September 18, 1937. About that first date, Ursula wrote that Howard's friends asked him if his new Olds had good pickup. "Absolutely," he said, "I'm taking this girl out Saturday night."

Howard worked at the General Motors plant until December 1944, when he and Ursula bought a grocery and meat market in Pontiac. The business was successful and they soon built a new store, with an apartment for themselves, next door to the old one. Howard would operate the store until 1976, when he retired at age 70. Howard and Ursula had a son, Barry, who was born on December 30, 1946. Barry later married Marchia Satkowiak and together they had two daughters: Wendy and Pamela. Howard died on January 2, 1984. Ursula still lives in Pontiac.

Ursula I. (Vincent) Wheeler (1918-) and Howard O. Wheeler (1905-1984) in 1943

Les left home in 1925 at the age of 16. With his cousins, Bert and Floyd, he left in a Model T Ford to seek his fortune out west. They made it to North Platte, Nebraska, when they ran out of money, sold the Model T, and decided to join the Navy. Bert and Floyd were shipped out to San Diego immediately while Les, who had to lie about his age, was held up in North Platte for awhile. It probably didn't help that Les was short in stature; in fact, his nickname was "Shorty." After basic training, the three Wheelers served together on the same ship, a destroyer named the U.S.S. Farquiry. Les later served on the U.S.S. San Francisco, and then the U.S.S. Enterprise (the "Big E"), an aircraft carrier which was probably the most famous ship of World War II. Les was a machinist in the Navy and was very good with a lathe. But during battles his job was to support the aircraft which landed on the Big E. Les sometimes told about how, during the Battle of Midway, when planes landed on the carrier he would pull dead gunners out and then help new gunners climb in before the plane took off again.

Leslie E. Wheeler (1909-1973)

Alexandria Man's Ship Reported Sunk Six Times

Leslie E. Wheeler, (above), of Alexandria is a chief machinist's mate aboard the carrier USS Enterprise, which returned to the States after 19 months of combat in the Pacific. Chief Wheeler, veteran of 18 years' naval service, has been aboard the famed "Big E" during the last 26 months. Reported by the Japs as sunk at Pearl Harbor, and at least six times since, the Enterprise has participated in every island invasion from Guadalcanal to Okinawa.

Chief Wheeler's wife and daughter, Arline, 4, live in Alexandria.

Les retired from the Navy as a Warrant Officer after World War II was over. He spent most of his twenty plus years of service at sea. During the war he married Leocadia M. Montero, who was called "Lulu," on November 28, 1942 in Hawaii. Lulu was born in Maderia, Portugal on April 21, 1905, and arrived in the Hawaiian Islands with her family in 1906. Her mother's name was Maria and her father, Manuel, worked in the sugarcane fields. Lulu was one of 14 children, including two pairs of twins. Lulu married Edward Augustus Kahele at age 16 on November 9, 1921. He was 32 and a full-blooded Hawaiian. They were married for only two and one-half years when Edward died on February 10, 1924, of a liver problem. They had two children: a stillborn boy followed by a girl named Lulu Apoleilani Kahele, who was born on August 17, 1923. The younger Lulu was called "Sweetie" and in 1939 she married Ervin Eugene Johnson, who was originally from North Carolina but was stationed in Hawaii as a soldier in the Army. Together they had a daughter, Arlene, who was born on October 11, 1940.

It isn't known how or when Les met Lulu. Lulu claimed she was at Pearl Harbor on December 7, 1941, when it was attacked by the Japanese. Shortly after they married they adopted Lulu's granddaughter, Arlene. The reason for the adoption is unclear, but it appears that at the time Sweetie was unable to properly care for Arlene. Sweetie is currently living in Hawaii and is married to Ernest Akim Seu. After Arlene, Sweetie had eight more children with her first husband before they divorced, and one daughter with Ernest. In the early 1950s, Les and Lulu tried to adopt more of Sweetie's children but were unsuccessful. They did not have any children of their own.

After retiring from the Navy, Les and his family moved back to Clarissa. Les was in the Navy for over 20 years and had a difficult time adjusting to civilian life. He received a good pension from the Navy but seemed to spend the money as fast as he got it. Les was a heavy drinker and this used up a lot of money. But Les was also very generous: when home on leave he always brought candy and gifts to Ted's children.

Leocadia M. (Montero) Wheeler (1905–1991), Arlene (Wheeler) Stapf (1940–) and Lulu A. (Kahele) Seu (1923-)

Les enjoyed fishing and hunting and didn't pay much attention to the game laws. He once soaked shelled corn and rye in whiskey and then spread the grain out on a field where Canadian geese were known to land during their migration. The geese landed, ate the grain, became intoxicated and couldn't fly. Les said he just walked out and picked them up.

Les was also known as a prankster. Once, while Les was at the Reuter farm visiting Ted and Margaret, one of the cows died and Margaret asked Ted what had caused it. Les went out to the cow, cut it open, removed the intestines and then mixed them up with a bucket filled with old rusty bolts. He brought the bucket to the house and explained to Margaret that the cow must have died after eating the bolts.

By the mid-1950s, Les, Lulu, and Arlene had left Clarissa and settled in Everett, Washington. Arlene married John Hollowick in 1956 at age 16. Together they had two children: Brent Eugene in 1957 and Gina Lee in 1958. Arlene was divorced in 1960 and remarried in 1961. She had three daughters with her second husband before they divorced in 1970. Les and Lulu now had a lot of grandchildren to enjoy. Les owned a boat and did some commercial fishing while in Washington. He died from a heart attack on September 29, 1973, at age 64. Lulu lived to age 86, spending the last several years with her granddaughter Gina. She died from heart problems on December 15, 1991.

In the 1930s, farming became a very difficult occupation. The Depression began on Black Friday, October 29, 1929, when the stock market crashed. The Dow Jones Industrial Average, which had reached a high of 381.2 in 1929, fell to 198.7 later that year. In 1932, the high for the DJIA was 88.8. Large numbers of investors lost everything and many businesses went bankrupt. The unemployment rate went up to 25 percent and many people went to soup kitchens for food. The farm economy also suffered. Bumper crops caused grain prices to drop significantly, which eventually caused many farmers to lose their land. Then the drought of 1933 and 1934 came. Much of the Midwest had no rain for up to nine months at a time. Dust storms began in Texas and Oklahoma, but eventually spread to the upper Midwest. Dust was everywhere: it accumulated along fences and crept into houses. Many people left farming and the Midwest and moved to California.

Will is remembered as a happy man who enjoyed deer hunting and who took his children and grandchildren fishing on nearby lakes. He also enjoyed playing whist and cribbage and listening to the radio. However, he must have had some unhappy periods as well. With the Depression and the drought, farming must have seemed a very hopeless way to make a living.

Will took his own life in the barn on the morning of Christmas Eve, December 24, 1938. The article below mentions that Herman Klug, the hired man, discovered Will in the barn, but it was actually Will's daughter Dorothy.

Will died intestate, or without a will. The family held an auction of the livestock and farm equipment which netted over $3,000. But after paying off debts and funeral expenses, Bertha and Dorothy were left with $750.

Dorothy was 16 when her father took his life. She finished high school, trained to become a telephone operator, and was married in 1940. The farm was leased out and later sold in 1944 for $7,200. This was $45 per acre (160 acres), including the buildings. Bertha received approximately $3,000 from the sale, while Will's sons and Dorothy each received $1,000. Bertha eventually was remarried to Mike Terek, and lived for awhile in California. She died in 1978, and is buried at the Sunset Memorial Cemetery in Alexandria.

Carlos Farmer Takes His Life

Wm. A. Wheeler Found Dead in Barn with Self-Inflicted Bullet in Head

Wm. A. Wheeler, 60, well-known Carlos township farmer, was found dead in the store-room of the barn on the Wheeler farm on Highway 29 north of Carlos by the hired man, Herman Klug, about 9:00 o'clock Saturday morning, with a bullet wound in his head.

Dr. J. A. McCabe was called and found that Mr. Wheeler had taken his own life with a 32-caliber revolver. The bullet entered his right temple.

He had been in poor health for some time and it is thought that this prompted the rash act. He leaves a wife and four children.

Mr. Wheeler was a well known and respected citizen of the Carlos community and his tragic death was a great shock to everybody who knew him.

William Henry Wheeler was born in Carlos township, the son of pioneer settlers, on August 14, 1878. He grew to manhood there, attending the local schools, and had spent all of his life in that community.

He was married to Sarah Anderson, of Carlos. To this union three children were born: Lloyd Wheeler of Clarissa, Howard Wheeler of Pontiac, Michigan and Leslie Wheeler, who is in the U.S. Navy, located at Long Beach, Cal. Mrs. Wheeler passed away in 1911. He was married to Mrs. Bertha (Jacobs) Hublou November 15, 1920 and to this union one daughter Dorothy, was born.

She lives at home. A brother and three sisters also survive him: Ira Wheeler of Carlos, Lois Wheeler of Alexandria, Eva (Mrs. Bert Lund), who lives in California and Lottie (Mrs. Albert Darch) of Fargo.

Funeral services were held on Wednesday afternoon at 12:45 o'clock at the Anderson Funeral Home and at 1:30 o'clock at the Bethany Lutheran church at Carlos; Rev. C. E. Hansen officiating.

Burial was in the church cemetery at Carlos. The pall bearers were: Otto Gutzman, Albert Bartelt, Wm. F. Palmer, Mike Ritten, Nick Schlosser and Peter Streed.

A quartet composed of Mr. and Mrs. Sam Meyers, Wallace Gless and Mrs. Peter Beheng furnished the music, accompanied by Mrs. Chas. Anderson, singing "Only A Step to Jesus," "Nearer, Still Nearer" and "God Will Take Care Of You."

His children were all present at the services except Leslie of Long Beach, Calif.

From the Park Region Echo (December 29, 1938) of Alexandria, Minnesota.

AUCTION

The personal property of Wm. H. Wheeler will be sold at public auction, two and one-half miles northwest of Carlos on Highway No. 29—

Thursday, March 16

Sale Starts at 10 O'clock — Free Lunch at Noon

Cattle—High Grade, All T-B and Bangs Tested.

HOLSTEIN CATTLE—1—6 years old will be fresh Nov. 15; 2—4 years old will be fresh about time of sale; 3—6 years old will be fresh Nov. 17; 4—3 years old was fresh Feb. 10; 5—5 years old will be fresh April 5; 6—5 years old, red spotted cow to freshen Oct. 1; 7—5 years old was fresh Feb. 19; 8—3 years old will be fresh Oct. 10; 9—7 years old will be fresh Nov. 5; 10—2½ years old was fresh Jan. 25; 11—3 years old was fresh Jan. 20; 12—3 years old will be fresh Sept. 15; 13—4 years years old will be fresh September 1st; 14—4 years old was fresh February 1st; 1 Holstein heifer two years old will be fresh Aug. 1; 2 Holsteins and 1 Guernsey heifer, 14 and 16 months old; One A-1 cattle dog

HOGS and POULTRY—3 brood sows, 1 due first part of March, others latter part of April; 50 Leghorns and 30 Wyandotte Chickens

HAY and FEED—300 bu. barley; 300 bu. oats; 100 bu. corn; some hay in barn

HORSES—1 black gelding 8 years, weight 1400; 1 grey gelding 9 yrs., wt. 1500; 1 bay mare 12 years, to foal in April, wt. 1350; 1 grey gelding, 11 years, wt. 1500; 2 colts, 1 and 2 years old

MACHINERY—1 spring tooth harrow, McCormick-Deering; 2 road graders; 2 bob sleighs; 1 wood wheeled wagon; 1 steel wheel wagon with rack; 1 concrete mixer; 1 Superior fanning mill; 1 Letz feed mill; 1 feed cooker; 3 water tanks; Vega cream separator, like new; 2 pump jacks; 1 International 1½ h. p. gas engine; 1 Fairbanks Morse 3-horse engine; 1 cream cooler; 2 electric motors, ¼ h.p. each, practically new 2 sets harness; 1 rowboat; 1 scale; 1 brooder house; 1 brooder stove; 1—2-wheel trailer; 1 wood pile, mixed red oak and poplar; Chevrolet 1931 sedan; tools; post drill; grindstone; 1 post vise; blacksmith's forge; oil drums; forks; shovels; 1 grain binder, Deering 8 ft; 1 corn binder, McCormick-Deering; 2 single row cultivators, International; 1 Hayes corn planter with check wire; 1—2-row cultivator, McCormick-Deering, nearly new; McCormick mower, 5½ ft.; 2 hay rakes, 1 side delivery; 1 New Idea hay loader, like new; 1 McCormick-Deering manure spreader; 1 Aspinwall potato planter; 1 McCormick-Deering potato digger; 1 potato sprayer; 2 gang plows, Emerson; 2 walking plows; 1 breaking plow; 1 disc; 1 four section iron drag; 1 wood drag, 3 horse; 1 drag cart; Hammers, saws and other articles too numerous too mention.

HOUSEHOLD GOODS—Dining room table and chairs; 2 buffet; kitchen table; 2 rocking chairs; 3 beds and springs; 2 dressers; 1—300-egg incubator; 1—100 egg incubator; 1 Monarch kitchen range; 1—30 gal. jar; 1—20 gal. jar; 1—6 gallon jar; cooking utensils and things too numerous to mention; 1 brooder house, 12x14; 2-wheel trailer

TERMS—Sums under $10 cash. Over that amount time given on bankable paper. No goods to be removed until settled for.

Wm. H. Wheeler Est.

— JAMES HOVE, Administrator —

Carlos State Bank, Clerk — Herb L. Strong, Auctioneer

Auction bill for William H. Wheeler sale

IV. LLOYD H. & MARGARET M. WHEELER

LLOYD H. WHEELER
Family Tree

Lloyd H. Wheeler
Carlos, Minnesota
b. Dec. 18, 1906
d. Oct. 26, 1983

Margaret M. Green
Hamden, Missouri
b. April 5, 1906
d. Feb. 5, 1988

m. November 11, 1925

Lloyd J. Wheeler
Carlos, Minnesota
b. Dec. 11, 1926

Maybelle A. Lundgren
Eagle Bend, Minnesota
b. Feb. 23, 1930

m. Oct. 12, 1947

James H. Wheeler
Carlos, Minnesota
b. Sep. 17, 1928

Mona M. Murphy
Browerville, Minnesota
b. May 11, 1924

m. Nov. 25, 1951

***Shirley A. Eberspacher**
Belle River, Minnesota
b Oct. 28, 1931

Robert W. Swanson
Long Prairie, Minnesota
b. Dec. 6, 1930

m. Feb. 11, 1951

Beverly J. Swanson
Belle River, Minnesota
b. Sep. 8, 1934

Peter W. Swanson
Eagle Bend, Minnesota
b. May 1, 1934

m. Jan. 9, 1955

Bruce G.
Bertha, Minnesota
b. Feb. 18, 1949

Byron A.
Bertha, Minnesota
b. June 14, 1955

Deborah K.
Grand Island, Nebraska
b. June 23, 1959

Mary K.
Camp LeJeune, NC
b. Oct. 2, 1952

Sue A.
New Bern, North Carolina
b. Jan. 18, 1956

Pamela J.
New Bern, North Carolina
b. Aug. 9, 1957

William J.
Lexington, Nebraska
b. Aug. 11, 1961

Connie L.
Memphis, Tennessee
b. Nov. 9, 1952

Steven R.
Columbus, Nebraska
b. Feb. 7, 1956

Michael A.
North Platte, Nebraska
b. Oct. 30, 1958

Sarah A.
North Platte, Nebraska
b. Sep. 9, 1963

Mark D.
St. Cloud, Minnesota
b. Jan. 8, 1957

Lori L.
Grand Island, Nebraska
b. Sep. 26, 1959

Becky D.
Broken Bow, Nebraska
b. Dec. 14, 1960

Jeni L.
Grand Island, Nebraska
b. Sep. 13, 1970

---

*Shirley's second husband is Stanley A. Eberspacher, m. April 10, 1982.

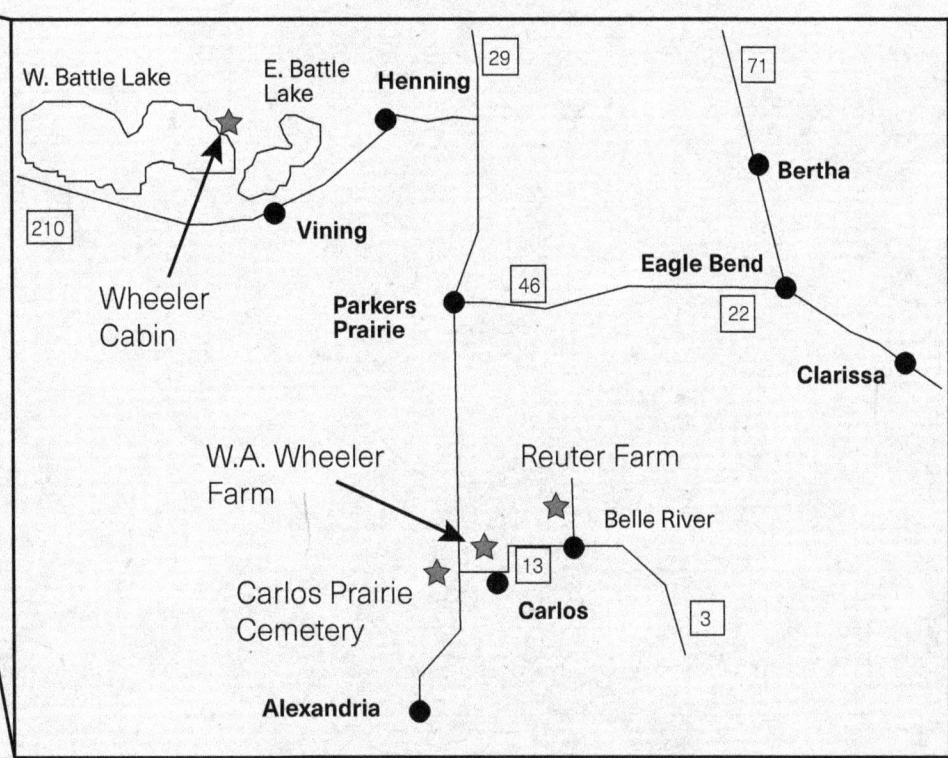

EARLY YEARS

Lloyd Henry Wheeler was born on December 18, 1906, on the Wheeler farm outside of Carlos. When he was a child, other kids called him "Ted" and for the rest of his life he was never called anything else. Many people at Ted's funeral were surprised to learn his real name was Lloyd. Ted was the second of three boys and just before he turned five, his mother Sarah died. Lois Wheeler, Ted's aunt, moved in with the family and helped raise the three boys. Ted went to school at District No. 69, the school his grandfather helped build. He received his diploma in 1922 at age 15.

In 1924, at age 17, Ted left his father's farm and went to Sioux City, Iowa, to look for work. While in Sioux City, Ted met a man named Chester Orwood and together they traveled through central Iowa looking for work picking corn. They ended up in Pioneer, Iowa, which today has a population of 46 and is about nine miles from Gilmore City, Iowa. Ted picked corn on a crew which included Albert and Elwood Green. Elwood eventually brought Ted to the Green family home outside of Gilmore City. Elwood's sister Maggie had just finished washing her hair as Elwood and Ted arrived, and she hid in the pantry so that Ted wouldn't see her. This is how Ted met his future wife, Margaret Marcella Green.

Margaret, who was called "Maggie" when she was young, was born on April 5, 1906, in Hamden, Missouri. She was the fifth of 12 children born to John William Green and Dora Beatrice Cook. John and Dora were raised in Missouri and after they married the family traveled around central Missouri as John searched for work. In 1912, John Green traveled to central Iowa and found farm work. In 1913, he returned to Missouri and moved the family to Gilmore City, Iowa by train. Today, Gilmore City has a population of 776. The Green family moved around a lot as John rented different farms in the area. John Green lived to the age of 94, dying in April 1952. Dora Green lived to age 90, dying in April 1957. In their later years, John and Dora moved from Iowa to Horton, Kansas, which is where they are buried.

A recent photo of the Green home outside Gilmore City, Iowa, where Ted Wheeler first met Margaret Green

John W. Green (1857-1952) with two grandchildren: Mary and Bernard Ryan

Dora B. (Cook) Green (1876-1957)

The Green children at the funeral of their mother, Dora, in 1957. From left to right; back row: Woodrow, Lawrence, Elwood, Albert, Virgil and Lonnie; front row: Leslie, Ida Mae, Lucinda, Margaret, and Calvin

John and Dora Green liked Ted and, as they were preparing to move again, offered him a job helping them move. This is when he really got to know Margaret. Ted began a new job on April 1, 1925, on a nearby farm for $40 per month. Ted and Margaret's courtship lasted all summer and into the fall. They were married on November 11, 1925, in Fort Dodge, Iowa. The attendants were Lucinda ("Sid") and Henry Niemar (Margaret's sister and brother-in-law) and the minister was Bertram M. Osgood.

Ted enjoyed telling the story of how he married Margaret one day and picked corn the next. In those days corn was picked by hand. A team of horses would pull a wagon along a row of corn. The picker, wearing what was called a husking hook on one hand, would walk between rows, snap ears of corn off the stalk, and throw them up into the wagon. The ears would hit a "bang board" and fall into the wagon box. A good corn picker could keep one ear in the air at all times. Corn pickers were paid by volume, getting anywhere from 1½ to 5 cents per bushel. Corn picking was considered to be very hard work.

Lloyd H. ("Ted") and Margaret M. (Green) Wheeler's wedding on November 11, 1925, in Fort Dodge, Iowa

Corn was an important element in the lives of our ancestors. The Wheelers and the Greens both raised corn and their relative prosperity often depended on the price of corn at that moment. Elwood Green, now 80 years old, has become a prosperous corn farmer. Elwood remembers corn getting as low as 8 cents a bushel in the early 1930s. Today it is about $2.50 per bushel, which is still low after adjusting for inflation, but farm productivity is much higher. A typical farmer can work a much larger piece of land and Elwood claimed that in some areas he now produced 200 bushels an acre without using irrigation. He estimated that an average yield in 1924 would have been 39 bushels per acre. Ted and Margaret would spend most of the next 12 years growing corn with limited success.

A wagon used for corn picking. It held 36 bushels of ear corn.

Elwood and Marie Green of Humboldt, Iowa

FARMING

In December 1925, Ted returned to Carlos and introduced Margaret to his family. Ted then rented the Wheeler farm from Will for the next three years. They had two sons while living at the Wheeler farm: Lloyd Joseph Wheeler was born on the farm on December 11, 1926, and James Henry Wheeler was born on September 17, 1928. Will decided to return to the farm soon afterward and Ted and Margaret then moved to Laverne, Iowa. Ted picked corn that winter and then worked on a nearby farm during 1929. The family moved to Fort Dodge the following year and Ted found work at a gypsum mill. Ted and Margaret put a down payment on a house in Fort Dodge, but then Ted was laid off and they lost the house. Losing that house bothered Ted for the rest of his life. Will then found a farm for Ted to rent near Belle River, Minnesota, which is seven miles from Carlos. The farm was owned by Frank Reuter, who also owned several other farms as well as a grocery store in Carlos. Ted and Margaret moved back to Minnesota in the fall of 1930 and settled in on the Reuter farm. The family would live there for the next seven years.

The farmhouse on the Reuter farm was two stories, with two bedrooms upstairs and a kitchen, living room, and bedroom where Ted and Margaret slept on the first floor. The house had no electricity or running water. The family used kerosene lanterns and gas lamps for light and carried pails of water to the house from an outside well. An outhouse served as the toilet, and the family used a catalog for toilet tissue. The house was heated by a pot-bellied stove in the living room and there was also a Monarch cook stove in the kitchen. Heat traveled to the second floor through an iron grate in the ceiling above the pot-bellied stove. Both stoves burned wood, which had to be split and carried in every night.

A recent photo of the Reuter farmhouse near Belle River, Minnesota

The Wheelers didn't have a radio but they did have an old fashioned telephone which hung on the wall. The phone was on a "party line," which meant that all the neighbors in the area shared the same line. You answered the phone depending on the number of rings, such as two long rings, two short rings, or one long and one short ring. Everyone on the party line heard the rings and would know who the call was for. People on the line could also eavesdrop on their neighbors' conversations. This was called "rubbering."

Ted and Margaret had two girls while on the Reuter farm: Shirley Ann Wheeler was born on October 28, 1931, and Beverly Jane Wheeler was born on September 8, 1934. Both girls were born in the first floor bedroom of the farmhouse. A midwife named Inger Christy helped Margaret with the births.

The children attended school in a one room schoolhouse (District No. 92), which was one mile from the farm. The school had wooden desks with ink wells that actually contained ink. The kids also went barefoot during the summer and on Saturday night took baths in a big wash tub in the middle of the kitchen. When a kid came down with a cold Margaret applied vapor rub around the neck at bedtime and then wrapped a cloth around it. She also doled out spoonfuls of cod liver oil.

The Reuter farm had approximately 160 acres. Besides the farmhouse there was a barn, silo and machine shed. Ted grew corn and oats, (and one year tried potatoes), and also had some dairy cows, pigs, chickens, a team of four mules, and two horses.

Operating a farm meant lots of hard work and everyone had a job to do, including the kids. For example, milking cows was a difficult job which had to be done every day. While Lloyd was squeezing out the milk, the cows would swing their tails back and forth and sometimes hit him in the face. Once in awhile a cow would kick over the milk bucket and Lloyd would lose all of his milk, along with his dignity. After the milking was done

Jim and Lloyd Wheeler on the Reuter farm around 1934.

it had to be separated in a Dela Valve Cream Separator. The milk was poured into a big bowl on top. The separator had a crank with a bell attached to it. When the crank was turned the bell rang until the crank was turning at the proper speed. When the bell stopped certain valves were then opened which permitted the whole milk to flow into the separator. The cream and the skim milk then came out of different spouts. Most of the skim milk was fed to the pigs and calves, but Ted took the cream to the creamery in Belle River. Most of the year he could drive to Belle River in his car, but during the winter he used what the family called the "Santa Claus Wagon." This was a bobsled which Ted had made some modifications to, including a little cab enclosure with a sheet of glass to shield the riders from the wind. The Santa Claus wagon was pulled by horses and the reins went through two holes in the dash. The cream cans had blankets over them to keep the cream from freezing. They also served as seats for Ted and the kids.

Another winter job was to add more insulation to the farmhouse. Ted would take a roll of building paper and, using slats, nail it to the outside of the house. He then piled manure from the barn against the paper (the manure would quickly freeze), which helped keep the house warm. In the spring, when things warmed up, the manure and paper were removed. Other never-ending jobs included cleaning the barn and chopping wood.

Ted bred and raised a team of four mules. A mule was the offspring of a mare horse and a "jack mule" (an ass or a donkey), and was difficult to break and train. Ted blindfolded a mule with a gunny sack while Margaret pinched the mule's lips with pliers. This would distract the mule so that Ted could get a harness on. Ted then trained the mule by hitching it to a set of horses. He used the mules in the field and also hitched them to a road grader to grade the local roads. Ted was proud of his four mule team and they were also admired by friends and neighbors. It's amazing to think that Ted and Margaret used a mule team for farming and also saw men walk on the moon.

But life on the farm wasn't all work. On weekends, the family went into Carlos and in the summer watched baseball games. The kids would stop by their Uncle Ed Fenske's garage, where he gave them each a nickel for an ice cream cone or candy. Ted also brewed his own beer (despite Margaret's objections) and rolled his own cigarettes. The family socialized with the neighbors, including the Zimmels and the Steidls. Ted and Margaret visited and played whist with them. Christmas was also a special time. The family always had a tree, which was decorated with tinsel and real candles.

CLARISSA

In 1937, Ted and Margaret decided to give up farming and try something else. It was a difficult way to make a living. Farming itself was full of hardships, but when combined with the Depression, drought, and raising a family, it must have been a very trying time. Ted and Margaret were sharecropping one of Frank Reuter's farms and for most of the year they ran a bill at Reuter's grocery store in Carlos. When the crops came in there was often barely enough money to pay off the grocery bill. One summer, they even canned dandelion greens to eat the following winter. Ted was also having trouble with his back, which made heavy farm work difficult. Ted confided to a neighbor, Mark Steidl, that things were not going well and that he had to do something else. But in the 1930s, in rural Minnesota, with four small children to clothe and feed, the opportunities must have seemed few and far between.

Ted's uncle, Ole Anderson, owned a restaurant and beer tavern in Carlos. Ted told Ole that he would like to buy the business from him if Ole ever wanted to sell; however, Ole later sold the business to someone else. Ted was disappointed, but this made him and Margaret more determined than ever to change their circumstances. They traveled around to nearby towns and in Clarissa, 35 miles northeast of Carlos, they found a restaurant for sale. Neither Ted nor Margaret had any experience running a restaurant, but this apparently did not stop them. We don't know how long they thought about it, or how much they paid, but we do know they bought the restaurant from Martha Rising and took possession on September 1, 1937. In August 1937, they auctioned off their farm equipment and livestock, packed up their remaining possessions, and moved to Clarissa. Ted and Margaret were 30 and 31 years old, respectively. Lloyd was 10, Jim was eight, Shirley was five, and Beverly was two.

PUBLIC AUCTION

Having decided to quit farming, I will sell at Public Auction at my place 1½ miles north and ¾ mile west of Belle River store on the old Nick Beheng farm, on—

Tuesday Aug. 31

Free Lunch at Noon — Sale starts at 10 o'clock A. M.

— CATTLE —

Holstein cow, 4 yrs. old, freshen Sept. 15
Guernsey cow, 8 yrs. old, freshened June 20
Holstein cow, 5 yrs. old, to freshen March 25
Holstein cow, 4 yrs. old, to freshen Sept. 24
Guernsey cow, 5 yrs. old, to freshen Sept. 29
Guernsey cow, 8 yrs. old, to freshen Sept. 20
Holstein cow, 4 yrs. old, to freshen Dec. 1
Holstein cow, 5 yrs. old, to freshen Oct. 12
Guernsey cow, 5 yrs. old, to freshen Sept. 24
Guernsey heifer, 2 yrs. old, to freshen Nov. 12
Guernsey heifer, 2 yrs. old
9 head Hereford feeders, ranging from 500 to 600 lbs.

— HORSES —

1 black horse, weight 1250; 1 buckskin mare, weight 1150
1 brood sow to farrow Aug. 31; about 20 Leghorn hens

— FEED —

About 6 acres of standing corn; about 13 ton alfalfa hay; around 9 ton of meadow hay; about 75 bushels barley; about 250 bushels oats.

— MACHINERY —

Deering corn binder; 6 ft. grain binder; Moline gang plow; John Deere corn planter, new; Van Brunt drill, 14 disc; Minnesota 2 row cultivator, new; John Deere single row cultivator; two sleighs; truck wagon, new; hay rack; manure spreader; McCormick-Deering hay rake; Deering mower; McCormick-Deering spring tooth; 15 ft. drag; cream separator; drag cart; 2 wheel stock trailer; 1½ horse gas engine; pump jack; 8 in. feed mill; grindstone; 2 sets work harness; Other articles too numerous to mention.

— HOUSEHOLD GOODS —

Leather davenport; library table; kitchen cupboard; Estate heatrola; 2 leather rockers; linoleum rug, 12x12.

TERMS—All sums under $10, cash. Over that amount time will be given on bankable paper. Anyone desiring credit must make arrangements with the clerk before the sale, otherwise he will be considered a cash buyer. No goods to be removed until settled for.

LLOYD WHEELER, Owner

Herb L. Strong, Auctioneer   First State Bank Carlos, Clerk

Auction bill for Ted and Margaret Wheeler's farm sale in 1937

Clarissa is located in Todd County, which is almost in the center of the state of Minnesota. The town was founded in 1877 by Louis and Clarissa Bischoffsheim of London, England, and named in her honor. Clarissa became more developed after the Great Northern railroad went through in 1883, and in 1904 the Eagle Valley Creamery Association was formed, which was the largest employer in Clarissa for many years.

However, Clarissa has remained a small town. The current population is about 650 people. When the Wheelers moved to town in 1937 the population was about 500. There are seven churches, three small manufacturing facilities, one weekly newspaper, and one well-kept main street. Ted and Margaret lived in Clarissa for 18 years and operated five different business during that period. They raised four children, and each of these children grew up, graduated from high school, met their spouse, and were married in Clarissa. They all consider Clarissa to be their home town.

The restaurant, which Ted and Margaret named "Wheeler's Inn," was located on Main Street, adjacent to the City Park. It was a long, narrow two-story building, one of the oldest in Clarissa. As you entered the building from the front entrance there was a bar area to the left where Ted served beer, straight ahead was a lunch counter with stools and several booths, and to the right was a stairway which led upstairs. Past the lunch counter and through a swinging door was the kitchen where the Wheeler family ate its meals.

Behind the kitchen was Ted and Margaret's bedroom and a back stairway. The basement housed a coal-fired steam furnace, which heated the entire building, while the upstairs consisted

The Wheeler family in Clarissa in 1943. From left to right: first row, Ted and Margaret; second row, Lloyd, Beverly and Shirley; third row, James.

of approximately 10 sleeping rooms. Lloyd and Jim shared one bedroom while Shirley and Beverly shared another. Lucy Berczyk, the town's postmistress, and her son Donald lived in a small group of rooms at the rear of the second floor. Ted and Margaret rented out the other rooms to people who might stay one night or a week. The rent was maybe $1.00 per night.

The restaurant was hard work. Ted and Margaret were on their feet for long periods waiting on customers. Ted kept the bar open till midnight while Margaret did the laundry for the upstairs rooms and, at the same time, acted as cook and waitress. Many of the teachers from the local schools who weren't married ate their meals at the restaurant. Margaret was often annoyed with their complaints about the food and service.

It's unclear how profitable the restaurant was for Ted and Margaret. (Ted always said "It wasn't how much money you made. It was how much money you *saved* that mattered.") The beer sales were strong, but the rest of the business was probably difficult. One indication of profitability may have been how often the restaurant changed hands after Ted and Margaret sold it in 1942. It was called Ma's Cafe (the Neises); The Pantry (the Carltons); The Idle Hour; Wally & Jerry's; The Park Cafe; The Top Notch Cafe (the Kopp girls); and the Do Drop Inn (the Thompsons). The building burned down in March 1977.

Margaret Wheeler and an unknown woman behind the counter at Wheeler's Inn

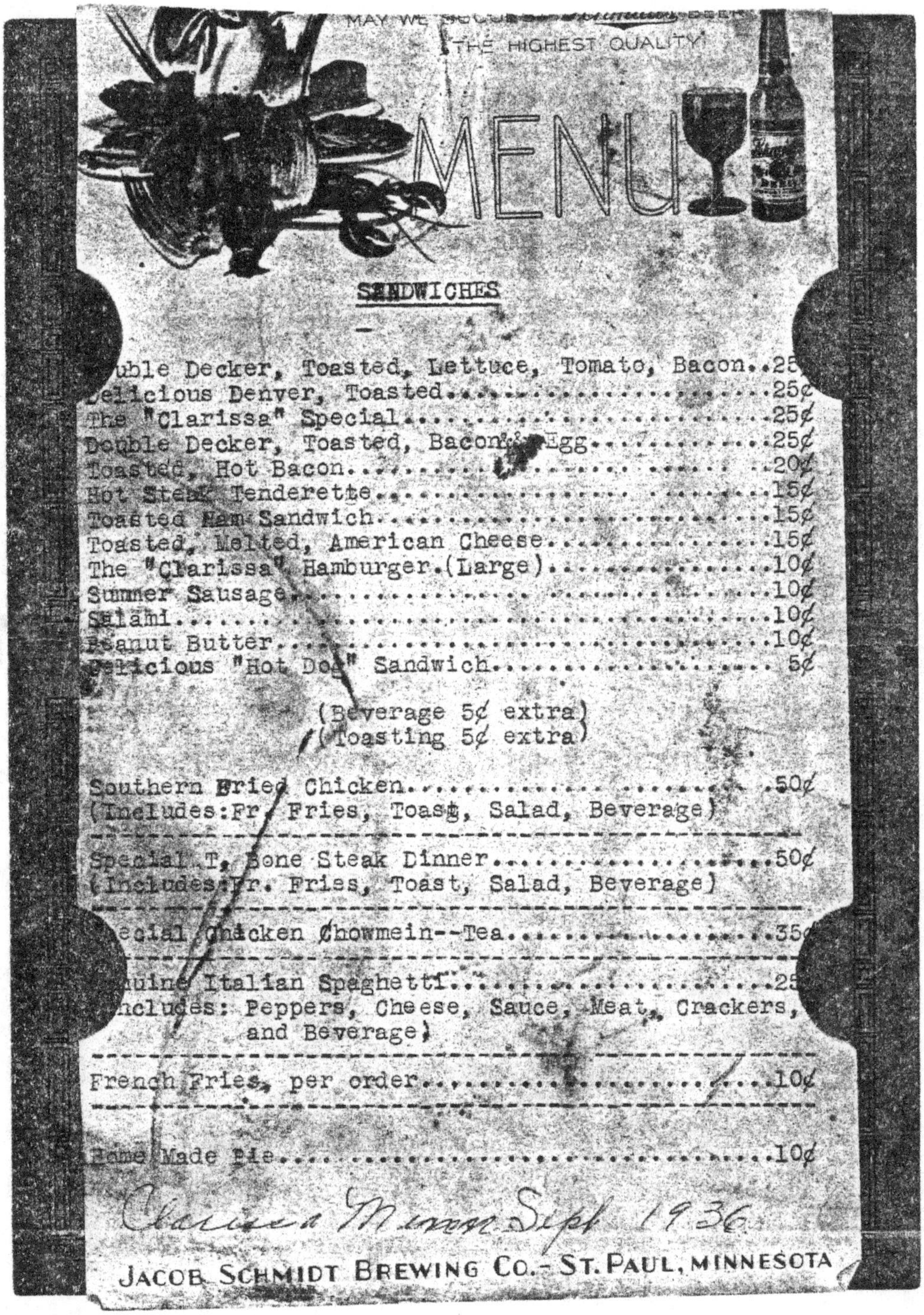

MENU

SANDWICHES

Double Decker, Toasted, Lettuce, Tomato, Bacon	25¢
Delicious Denver, Toasted	25¢
The "Clarissa" Special	25¢
Double Decker, Toasted, Bacon & Egg	25¢
Toasted, Hot Bacon	20¢
Hot Steak Tenderette	15¢
Toasted Ham Sandwich	15¢
Toasted, Melted, American Cheese	15¢
The "Clarissa" Hamburger (Large)	10¢
Summer Sausage	10¢
Salami	10¢
Peanut Butter	10¢
Delicious "Hot Dog" Sandwich	5¢

(Beverage 5¢ extra)
(Toasting 5¢ extra)

Southern Fried Chicken ... 50¢
(Includes: Fr. Fries, Toast, Salad, Beverage)

Special T. Bone Steak Dinner ... 50¢
(Includes: Fr. Fries, Toast, Salad, Beverage)

Special Chicken Chowmein--Tea ... 35¢

Genuine Italian Spaghetti ... 25¢
(Includes: Peppers, Cheese, Sauce, Meat, Crackers, and Beverage)

French Fries, per order ... 10¢

Home Made Pie ... 10¢

Clarissa Minn Sept 1936

JACOB SCHMIDT BREWING CO. - ST. PAUL, MINNESOTA

A menu from Wheeler's Inn. The date on the menu is September 1936, so it may have been from when Martha Rising owned the restaurant.

Hooty, The Wise Owl, Says—
Always Go To
WHEELER'S INN
For Good Food and Drinks
Schmidt's Beer On Tap — Coffee
Lunches — Dinners — Rooms
"Where All Good Fellows Meet"
Clarissa, Minn.

A blotter card for Wheeler's Inn

During the time they owned the restaurant, Ted and Margaret also owned a "lunch wagon," which resembled a two-wheel mobile home where one side opened out into a counter. They hauled the lunch wagon to farm auction sales to sell coffee, soda, sandwiches, and candy. One of Ted's close friends in Clarissa was Clint Murphy, a local auctioneer. Clint, as the auctioneer, would suggest to the farmer that he use Ted and Margaret's lunch wagon to provide "free lunches" to attract more people to the auction. On the day of the auction, Ted and Margaret woke the kids up at five a.m. to help prepare 300 to 500 of these free lunches, which consisted of one thin slice of bologna on a bun and coffee from a tin cup. Ted and Margaret also took the lunch wagon to the Todd County Fair in Long Prairie or to Clarissa baseball games.

Jim Wheeler in front of the lunch wagon. The man on the left is unknown.

In addition to the restaurant and the lunch wagon, Ted and Margaret also gave dances during this period. They first began to hold dances in the community hall, which was on the second floor of Bishop's Department Store just down the street from Wheeler's Inn. Lloyd and Jim ran the coat check room and were kept busy. There was no alcohol served in the community hall so patrons were always retrieving their coats to take a nip from the bottles in their pockets. In June 1940, Ted and Margaret purchased the Bertha Pavilion from Bill "Sharky" Paine for $500. The pavilion was located on the east edge of Bertha, a small town 14 miles north of Clarissa on Highway 71. Dances were very popular and because Ted could sell beer at the pavilion, it was a very profitable venture.

The pavilion was 75 feet wide and 80 feet long. The interior was very plain, with benches around the perimeter. There were large doors on each side of the building which could be opened in warm weather to catch the breeze. There were no inside bathrooms or even an outhouse at the pavilion. The men went behind the building to relieve themselves and the women went between the parked cars. But the pavilion did have a nice hardwood tongue and groove floor for dancing, and also roller skating. Roller skating was on Friday night and then on Saturday a special wax was applied to the floor for the dance that evening. During the week, the Wheeler kids and their friends cleaned the pavilion and scrubbed off the wax before the next Friday.

The dances had live music, usually from a local band. There was Gust Drong and the Blue Derbies from Browerville, Minnesota. They played polkas, waltzes, and foxtrots. One of the most popular bands at that time was The Six Fat Dutchman from New Ulm, Minnesota. They were famous for their polkas. The bands supplied Ted and Margaret with dance bills, which they then posted in Clarissa and nearby towns. The bands generally were paid based on a percentage of ticket revenues, but Ted made most of his money on the sale of beer. The Wheeler kids worked behind the bar, even though none of them were 21. Around 1946, the city of Bertha elected a new town council, which decided not to issue a beer license to Ted or the Bertha Pavilion. So Ted had the building cut into three pieces and moved to the outskirts of Clarissa. The building was renamed the Clarissa Ballroom and was just as successful as it had been in Bertha. Ted eventually sold the building in the late 1940s to Bill and Ruth Kulick, who remodeled the place and operated it for many years afterward. The Clarissa Ballroom is still standing, and the 7th Annual, three-day-long, Polka Fest was held at the Clarissa Ballroom over Memorial Day weekend in 1994.

Recent photo of the Clarissa Ballroom

In the 1940s and 1950s, a weekly column entitled "I Like It Here," written by George Grim, appeared in the Minneapolis Tribune. Grim featured the town of Clarissa several times in this column and the phrase "We Like It Here" became the town's unofficial slogan.

Clarissa has changed very little since the Wheelers lived there. The two photos on the next page are of Clarissa's Main Street. The top photo, which is probably from the 1960s, was taken fac-

ing east from the intersection of Main and Robert Streets. The building farthest to the left is Bishop's Department Store. The second floor was the community hall where Ted and Margaret first began holding dances. Three buildings down on the left is the Do Drop Inn. This was formerly Wheeler's Inn, the business Ted and Margaret first operated when they moved to Clarissa. The bottom photo, which is probably from the early 1940s, was taken facing west from the intersection of Main and Bridge Streets. The second building on the left, with the Dodge-Plymouth sign, is Wheeler's Sales & Service, which Ted and Margaret purchased in 1945 and operated until 1955.

Clarissa's Main Street, facing east

Clarissa's Main Street, facing west

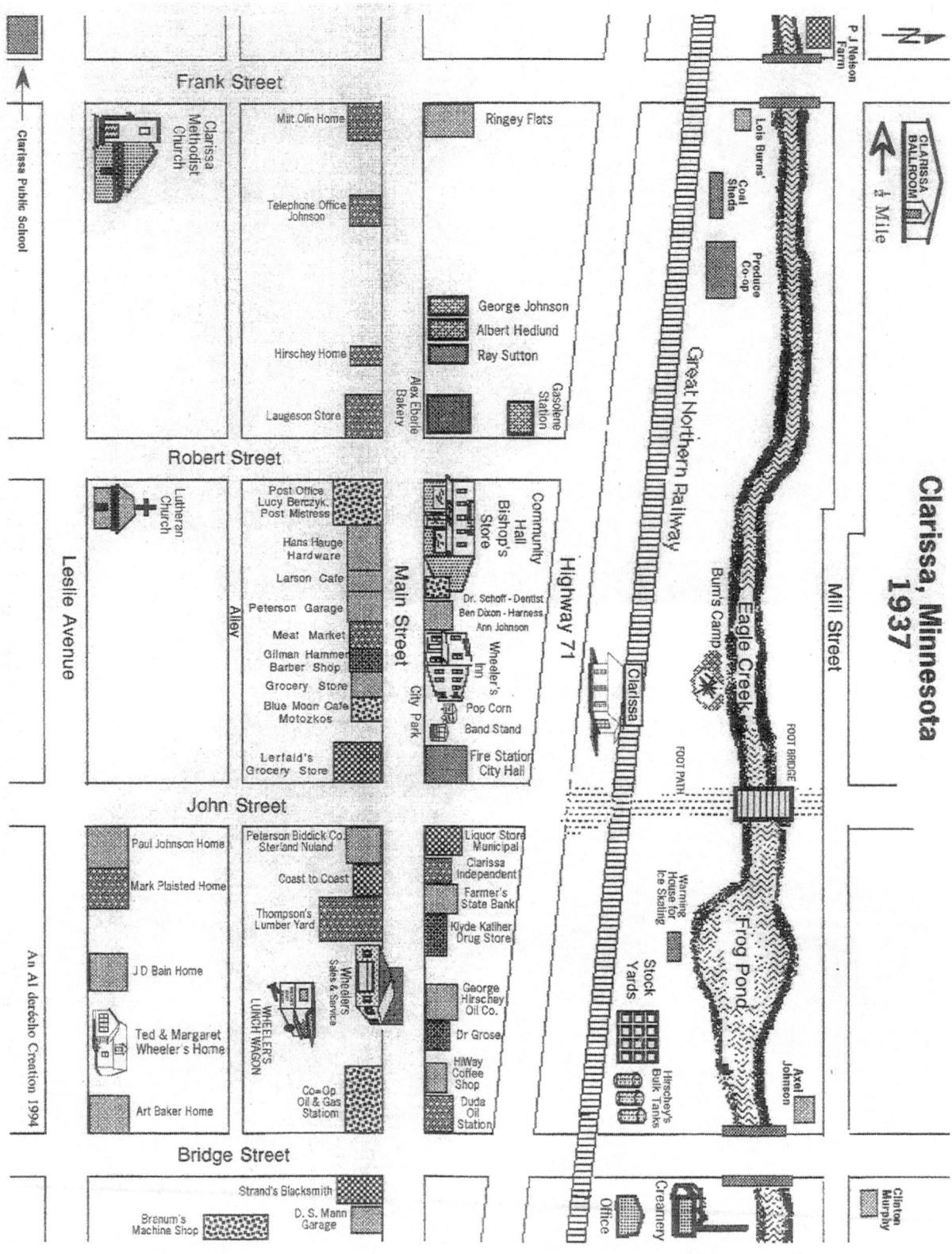

The drawing on the previous page has captured much of Clarissa in a four square block area. The town was actually larger than this but not by much. Almost every building highlighted in this drawing holds at least one memory for the Wheeler family. Heading west down Main Street:

The Strand's Blacksmith shop always had a special aroma.

Across the street, Ted worked at the Co-op Oil station from 1942 to 1945. He spent a lot of time repairing tires and tubes because new tires were scarce during World War II. In fact, gasoline was rationed during the war mainly to reduce consumption of rubber.

Across Main Street was Bill Duda's service station where all the Wheeler kids picked up newspapers for their paper routes. Ted and Margaret made sure the kids made their deliveries and collections on time. Once, Shirley spent her money before she paid off the newspaper. To punish Shirley, who was then about 12 years old, Margaret spanked her with a sewing machine belt. Today, Shirley has Margaret's old sewing machine.

Next door to Dudas was the HiWay Coffee Shop (or Lois' Cafe), where Shirley and Beverly both worked as waitresses.

Dr. Grose's office was in the first floor of the next building to the west. Dr. Grose was the most respected man in Clarissa—no one ever said a word against him. He cared for the whole community and often wasn't paid for his services. When Ted owned the garage, he used the wrecker to take Dr. Grose out in the country to make house calls during the winter.

Across the street from Dr. Grose's was Wheeler's Sales & Service, which Ted purchased in 1945. This will be described in greater detail later.

Shirley and Beverly Wheeler in Clarissa around 1939

Farther up the block was Kaliher's drug store, where the kids stopped after school for a 10 cent peanut double.

Two doors up was the Clarissa Independent, which was owned by the Etzells. The paper came out once a week and a good portion of it was devoted to the social activities of the town. A reporter called each family once a week to ask if they had any news. The Wheelers would report each month that they went to Alexandria to visit Aunt Lois. The name of the paper has changed, but it still carries this social column.

Next door was the liquor store, which no respectable woman entered.

In the next block was the City Hall and Fire Station, which makes one think of Alex Knutson. Alex was sort of the town derelict: he drank a lot of beer and slept in the Fire Station. Alex had come to Clarissa some 30 years earlier and worked for nearby farmers grubbing out land with dynamite. He had no home or family and no permanent job. A group of townspeople, possibly the town council, decided that Alex should be put into an asylum in Fergus Falls, Minnesota. Ted and Margaret wouldn't hear of this, so instead they fixed up a place for him in the garage. In the winter Alex lived in the Wheeler basement. The kids cleaned his room and sometimes found half empty bottles of beer. Alex plugged the bottle with a wad of paper so the beer wouldn't go flat. He lived in this manner until he died around 1950.

Next door in the City Park was a bandstand where concerts were held on Wednesdays and Saturdays during the summer. People sat on benches, or in their cars with the windows rolled down, and listened to the band. Jim and Lloyd had a stand in the park from which they sold popcorn for a nickel a bag. One brother stayed in the stand to make popcorn and take care of the walk up traffic while the other walked around the park with a cardboard box full of bags of popcorn. The business was profitable but the season was short.

A popcorn stand similar to the one operated by Lloyd and Jim Wheeler

Wheeler's Inn was on the other side of City Park and has been described in detail earlier. There was a radio on the lunch counter where everyone gathered if there was a big event. A big crowd listened as Joe Louis knocked out Max Schmeling on June 22, 1938. There was a really big crowd on June 8, 1941, when President Roosevelt declared war against Japan the day after the attack on Pearl Harbor.

Next door to the restaurant was Ben Dixon's harness and shoe shop. If you got a hole in your shoe you took it into Ben's and he re-soled it for you. The smell of leather in his shop stayed with you for a long time.

Ann and Lyle ("Pickey") Johnson lived behind Dixon's. Lyle had infantile paralysis but even though he was crippled he still led a good life and always had a positive attitude. He died in 1993 of a heart attack.

Next door to Dixon's was Dr. Schoff, the dentist. If you were scared, his wife Elaine would put on a hand puppet to make you laugh.

Across the street from Wheeler's Inn was the Clarissa Meat Market. Jim worked here while he was in high school. Margaret thought he might become a butcher.

Bishop's Department Store was on the corner and it sold groceries, dry goods, and a little bit of everything. The ceiling and walls were covered with tin.

Across the street was the post office, where Lucy Berczyk was the postmistress.

In the next block was the telephone company's office. Darlene Swanson, one of the operators, let the kids rubber (listen) in on calls.

At the end of the block was Ringey Flats, which was Clarissa's low-income district.

Clarissa's Main Street was like the main street in all small towns. It was decorated with lights during the Christmas season; shop windows were covered with soap on Halloween; and there was a parade on the Fourth of July and another one on Memorial Day. After World War II, Lloyd and Wayne Murphy marched in the Memorial Day parade in their old uniforms, which at the time still fit them.

It isn't in the drawing, but a movie theater later opened in Clarissa. Ted was head of the fire department at the time and was asked to make a speech on opening night. His speech, in its entirety, was "damn nice thing for the town." A ticket for the movies cost 12 cents.

One block north of Main Street was Highway 71. Five miles to the west was Eagle Bend where everyone went to the movies until Clarissa got its own theater. Five miles to the east was Browerville, where Lloyd and Jim rode their bikes to play pool. Clarissa didn't have a pool hall.

Ted and Margaret had two serious car accidents on Highway 71 between Clarissa and Bertha. Coming home late one night after locking up the Bertha Pavilion, they missed a curve and went into a swamp. Going to Bertha with Lois Burns, Irene Johnson, and Bonnie Nelson they were hit by a lumber truck on the right side and rolled several times. In both accidents the cars were destroyed but no one was seriously injured.

The Great Northern railway ran parallel to Highway 71. Lloyd and Jim sometimes hunted pheasants with Don Fearing along the railroad tracks outside of town. They used Leo Cuchna's pointer, Sparky.

Between the railroad tracks and Eagle Creek was the Bum's Camp. Hobos came into town riding boxcars on the trains and lived for awhile in the camp before moving on. The Wheeler boys and their friends often went down to the camp and listened to their stories. It was also a good place for them to smoke cigarettes without fear of getting caught.

Eagle Creek ran next to the railroad tracks and there was a wide spot in the creek called Frog Pond. The kids fished in Eagle Creek but all they ever caught were small Northern Pike. The kids also swam in Eagle Creek as well as a place called Bare Lake. Frog Pond froze over in winter and the kids went ice skating as well as sliding on the Foot Bridge hill.

Clarissa's stockyards were a great place to play tag or have rubber band gun fights.

The Eagle Valley Creamery was on Bridge Street just north of Highway 71. Local farmers brought in their cream at least twice a week and the cream was then turned into butter. The creamery produced approximately one million pounds of butter each year, packaged under the brand name Louella, and sold it to American Stores in

The Eagle Valley Creamery in Clarissa, Minnesota

Philadelphia. Now the creamery is closed and milk is picked up at the farm by trucks from a plant in Browerville which is owned by Kraft Foods.

North of the creamery, on Mill Street, was Clint Murphy's home. Clint Murphy and Ted were good friends and the Murphy kids were friends with the Wheeler kids. Jim Wheeler married Mona Murphy in 1951. Jim and Wayne Murphy started a mink farm in an old building behind the Murphy home. The plan was to breed and raise minks, which were prized for their fur. They had up to 40 minks in pens, but the difficult part was feeding them. Jim and Wayne bought old horses, shot them, and then butchered them. The horse meat was ground up and fed to the minks.

South of Main Street was Leslie Avenue. Ted and Margaret bought their first house at 104 Leslie Avenue from Alex Woodash in 1942, when they moved out of Wheeler's Inn.

Ted and Margaret Wheeler's house at 104 Leslie Avenue in Clarissa

On the northeast corner of Leslie Avenue and Frank Street was the Methodist Church. The Wheelers went to church and Sunday School each Sunday. Ted didn't always join them but said that it was important to give to the church because it was like a business and needed funds to operate. One of the Sunday School teachers, Elizabeth Oshlund, is remembered fondly. All of the Wheeler children were married in this church.

The Methodist Church in Clarissa, Minnesota

The Clarissa Public School was on the southwest corner of Leslie Avenue and Frank Street. All the Wheeler kids graduated from high school here. Lloyd in 1945, Jim in 1946, Shirley in 1949, and Beverley in 1953. Lloyd and Jim both played six man football.

In the early summer of 1944, while working at the Co-Op Oil Station, Ted received a draft notice from the Army. After passing a physical, he was told to report to Fort Snelling in the Twin Cities. He put the house in Margaret's name and told his children to take care of their mother. His friends had a going away party for him and the minister came over for dinner. Lloyd was thinking of going into the service that fall and Ted said he would check it out and let Lloyd know if it was alright. Then Congress passed a law that said if you were going to be 39 or older by the end of 1944, you were exempt from the draft. Ted turned 39 on December 18, 1944, so he didn't have to go.

Lloyd joined the Navy in December 1944 with Wayne Murphy. He was 17 years old and in the middle of his senior year in high school. He and Wayne both got their diplomas anyway. Lloyd trained as an aviation radio operator on a PBM

The Clarissa Public School

patrol bomber, which was a seaplane used for search and rescue missions and anti-submarine warfare. He completed his basic training in Memphis, Tennessee and then was stationed in Florida, California and Washington. He never saw any action overseas and was discharged on July 15, 1946.

The Wheeler children in the mid-1940s: Lloyd, Beverly, Jim and Shirley

The garage on Main Street came up for sale in 1945. Ted wanted it badly and he bought it, though it isn't known for how much. The garage was a brick building which was about 55 feet wide and 75 feet long. It had big overhead doors at each end. In the front there was a small showroom with a counter and an office as well as an area for parts. Ted named the business Wheeler's Sales & Service.

At first the garage just did service work. Then Ted obtained a Dodge-Plymouth and Dodge Truck franchise in early 1946. He was a "sub-dealer," which meant he obtained his cars and trucks from larger dealers in Sauk Center and St. Cloud, Minnesota.

When Lloyd was discharged from the Navy, he went to work for Ted at the garage in the shop.

Wheeler's Sales & Service in Clarissa, Minnesota

He took a course in accounting in Minneapolis under the G.I. Bill and became the garage's bookkeeper. The first mechanics were Leonard ("Fat") Johnson and John Eckman. Later on, Herman Puhr and Elmer Winquist also worked in the garage. Shirley Wheeler worked in the office.

This ad appeared in The Clarissa Independent on January 17, 1946.

Working at Wheeler's Sales & Service, from left to right: Ted Wheeler, Shirley Wheeler, Lloyd Wheeler, Carl Carlson and Herman Puhr.

After the war new cars were difficult to get. The first new Plymouths that came in sold for less than $900. The cars had a suggested retail price, but many dealers sold them to whomever paid the highest price. Ted wouldn't charge more than list price. He sold his first car to Dr. Grose, whose office was just across the street. Dr. Grose needed a car to make house calls in the country. The second car he sold to Godfrey Nelson, the local rural mail carrier, and the third car was sold to his friend, Clint Murphy. In a town the size of Clarissa, there was not going to be a lot of new car sales but the garage did a lot of service work and a fair amount of business selling school buses.

Ted enjoyed the car business and was a good car salesman. He loved to deal and negotiate. He owned the garage until 1955, when he decided to go into the farm store business. Because the service work the garage did was sometimes charged, a lot of people owed Ted money. Ted said, "These are good people and they'll pay those bills." But when Ted decided to sell the garage, he and Lloyd went out to collect the accounts receivable. They didn't take in enough money to pay for the gas they were using up, so after three days they quit. Ted sold the garage to Leonard Johnson and Raymond Peterson. The garage later burned down in January 1978.

Ted and Margaret's children were growing up, getting married and moving away. Lloyd met Maybelle A. Lundgren of Eagle Bend in the fall of 1946 and married her on October 12, 1947. They had a son, Bruce, on February 18, 1949. Jim graduated from high school in 1946. He bought a dump truck and worked with it on various jobs for a year before going to Guam in 1948. He worked on Guam and Okinawa as a heavy equipment operator for almost four years before coming back to Clarissa and marrying Mona M. Murphy on November 25, 1951. He was then drafted into the Marine Corps. Shirley graduated from high school in 1949 and then worked at the garage. She married her high school sweetheart, Robert W. Swanson, on February 11, 1951. Bob had joined the Army along with Rodney Murphy and James Wodash, so he and Shirley left Clarissa for Texas soon after the wedding. Beverly graduated from high school in 1953 and went to Minneapolis to work in the office at Jones Press. She married Peter W. Swanson (Bob's cousin) on January 8, 1955, when he came home on leave from the Army and then returned with him to Texas as he completed his service.

The family at Ted and Margaret's home in Clarissa in 1951. From left to right: back row, Ted Wheeler, Margaret Wheeler, Mona (Murphy) Wheeler, Shirley (Wheeler) Swanson, Jim Wheeler, Lois Wheeler; front row, Beverly Wheeler, Bruce Wheeler, Lloyd Wheeler, Maybelle (Lundgren) Wheeler, Bob Swanson.

At the beginning of 1955, Ted and Margaret were both 48 years old. They had raised four children and now their children were starting families of their own. They were the owners of a successful business and were respected members of their community. It sounds like a happy ending to the story but in many ways it was just the beginning.

BATTLE LAKE

West Battle Lake has been a big part of the Wheeler's lives. Ted and Margaret built a cabin there in 1948 and spent every summer there from 1956 on. West Battle Lake was also the site of numerous vacations by Ted and Margaret's children and their families. Ted always said it was his favorite place in the world.

West Battle Lake is in Otter Tail County, approximately 40 miles west of Clarissa. The lake is named for a great Indian battle which took place along the winding creek between East and West Battle Lake. In 1795, a war party of fifty Ojibway from Leech Lake fought fiercely in a three day battle against a greater number of Sioux warriors. It's not clear who won.

West Battle Lake is a good-sized lake and is also very clean. It has an area of 5,600 acres and is up to 100 feet deep in several spots. When the wind blows hard the waves get too large for a typical fishing boat, and sometimes there's a morning fog which gets so thick you can lose your sense of direction. But it's really a very pleasant lake with many sandy beaches and a wooded shoreline. There are cabins around almost the entire perimeter of the lake and a number of small resorts. The lake mainly has sun fish and walleyes, but there are also northerns, crappies, large mouth bass, and some muskies.

In the early 1940s, a group of Clarissa men bought lots together along the northeast shore of West Battle Lake. The group included Ted Wheeler, Clint Murphy, Reno Lundquist, Clarence Grove, and possibly Joe Johnson. Each man bought a 50 foot lot for $50, except for Reno Lundquist, who purchased additional land. Later on the various areas around the lake were named and this particular area was called Clarissa Haven.

Ted's lot was 50 feet wide and approximately 400 feet deep and was full of trees and underbrush. He first grubbed out the lot and cleaned it up, just as he used to do back on the Reuter farm. In 1948, he built a cabin out of cinder block. It was 26 feet wide and 24 feet deep. In the beginning there was running water to the cabin but no toilets and also no electricity. Ted and Margaret used kerosene lamps for light and propane gas for cooking. After a couple years they got a septic tank and were also hooked up for electricity. Ted and Margaret used this cabin until the early 1970s, when they built a new cabin next door.

Ted and Margaret Wheeler in front of their old cabin at Battle Lake

Margaret and Ted Wheeler, with Heidi, in front of their new cabin at Battle Lake

There was a nice sandy beach in front of Ted and Margaret's place. You could walk out almost 100 yards without the water going over your head. Early in the summer the water was still pretty cold but when it warmed up Ted and Margaret enjoyed swimming.

Swimming at Battle Lake: back row, Margaret Wheeler, Ted Wheeler, Mona (Murphy) Wheeler, Jim Wheeler; front row, Shirley Wheeler, Beverly Wheeler.

In 1963, Ted built the boathouse down by the lake. It was 14 feet by 24 feet., made out of block and had a flat concrete roof so that Ted and Margaret could walk straight out from the cabin onto the roof and use it as a patio. There was a set of small trolley tracks which lead from the boathouse to the water. For many years Ted kept a large speedboat (with a wood hull) in the boathouse which he would gently roll down on a trolley to the lake using an electric winch and cable. Whenever anyone put the speedboat in the lake, it was always a dramatic moment, kind of like the launching of a ship.

Ted also had a fishing boat at the lake. In the early days it was a wooden boat with no motor. Ted used oars and would row out to where he wanted to fish. Later on, he had a nice boat with both a gas motor and an electric motor (for trolling). The fishing boat had a fancy lift which used an electric motor to raise the boat out of the water.

The boathouse at Battle Lake. Notice the trolley tracks leading down to the water.

Ted Wheeler raising the fishing boat out of the water using the electric motor

Ted liked to get up early to go fishing, so early that he would often be the only boat out on the lake. Ted always said that the early morning was the best time of the day. First he would fish for walleyes. His favorite bait for walleyes were minnows, although in later years he used leeches and nightcrawlers. He generally trolled, often with two lines, even though that was illegal in Minnesota. Sometimes he went to one of his favorite spots, shut off the motor and let the boat drift over a bar or a hole. After fishing for walleyes, he'd move over to a good spot for sun fish and anchor the boat. His bait for sun fish were angle worms and sometimes a little corn. When Ted came in from fishing, he always cleaned the fish right away down by the lake. Margaret often came down to the boathouse and helped him. The sun fish were scaled and the walleyes were filleted. He would roll the guts in newspaper, dig a deep hole, and bury them.

Ted Wheeler fishing on Battle Lake

Ted had a friendly rivalry about who caught the most fish with his cousin, Bert Wheeler, who had a cabin nearby. Ted fished early in the morning and Bert would kid him about this in front of others because he slept in and then fished in the late afternoon or early evening. One Sunday there was a group of people visiting on Ted and Margaret's patio and the topic turned to fishing. There were a number of stories about who caught this and who caught that, and eventually Pete Swanson asked Ted, "Tell me, who is the best fisherman on Battle Lake?"

Everyone got quiet and Ted thought about it for a moment. He finally said, "I really don't know, but his last name is Wheeler."

While he lived in Minnesota, Ted also went ice fishing in the winter. He often went on Sundays and usually took one of his sons or Reno Lundquist and Clint Murphy. Ted must have believed the old saying "It is better to go fishing and think about God than to go to church and think about fishing." Angling was allowed for ice fishing, but in those days most people speared for fish. Today, the opposite is true.

The house for spearfishing is a little larger than an outhouse, about four by four feet. There's a large hole in the floor, about 30 inches square, that also goes through the ice, which might be up to two feet thick. Today there are special drills to make the spearing hole but in those days they used a hammer or sledge and a chisel. The house usually has a little gas or wood stove and when the door is closed the inside of the house is dark. This allows the fisherman to see the bottom of the lake, 10 to 12 feet below, quite clearly. A decoy is then dropped through the hole on a fishing line. The fins on the decoy are adjusted so that when the line is pulled the decoy "swims" in a circle. Northerns sometimes rush in and grab the decoy, but usually they creep in next to the decoy to look at it more closely. That's when you spear them. Afterwards, the fish is tossed outside, and on a typical winter day in Minnesota it freezes immediately.

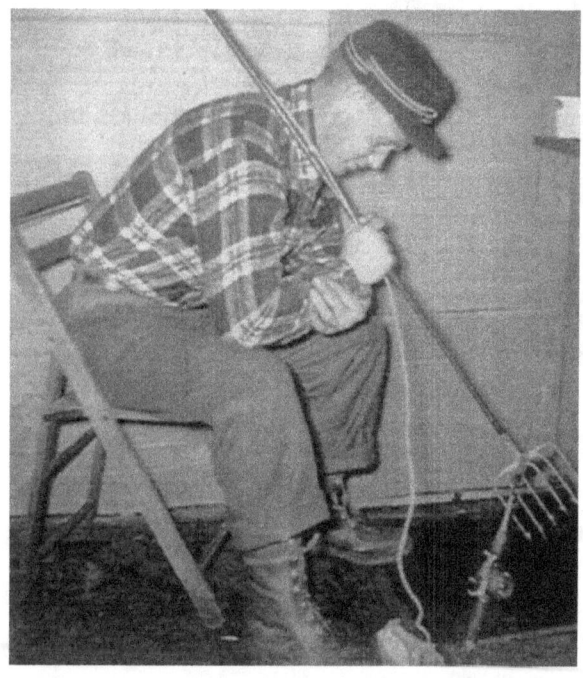

Jim Wheeler demonstrates his spear fishing technique

Jim Wheeler, Clint Murphy and Les Wheeler outside Murphy's spearing house on Battle Lake

When the ice became thick enough Ted would pull his house out on a toboggan. The house often stayed in the same place all winter and Ted and his friends usually put their houses next to each other. This led to the following article in the Clarissa paper:

Wow! What a Fish (Story)

Big Northern Speared In 3 Holes at Once

This story is told by three truthful (?) businessmen of Clarissa: C. A. Grove, Ted Wheeler, and Clinton Murphy.

One day last week they went spearing on Battle Lake. Each has a fish house on the lake, and they're neatly lined up about 15 feet apart.

Grove had his decoys set and was waiting. Along came the biggest Northern Pike he had ever seen, and up north, where he originally came from they have big ones (he says).

He threw his spear at it through the hole in the ice, but he got it in the tail. Pretty soon he heard a yell from Wheeler in his fish house 15 feet away. Wheeler had seen a big one too, had thrown his spear and got it in the Northern's back. That was no more than done, when Murphy let out a yell from his house 15 feet away. He'd thrown his spear and got a big one in the head.

A consultation was held by the three men. They figured they had speared the same fish. To get it out they had to chop a trench in the ice from Grove's fishhouse to Wheeler's to Murphy's (sounds like baseball, doesn't it?) to get the fish out.

* * *

Editor's note—Let's see, that would make a fish 30 feet long. Later: We checked on this and the fish they claim is 30 feet long measured 39 inches by tape, and weighed 13 pounds. It seems Wheeler speared it first, then called the others to come and spear it too in order to get it out—they just don't mention that all the spearing was done through the same hole in the ice.

This article appeared on the front page of The Clarissa Independent *on January 23, 1947.*

Margaret also enjoyed the lake. She didn't fish much but kept a vegetable and flower garden, as well as a number of birdfeeders. There were a lot of different varieties of birds at the lake, including hummingbirds, cardinals, and orioles.

Margaret Wheeler at Battle Lake

Ted and Margaret both played golf at the Balmoral golf course, which is located about eight miles from their cabin at Battle Lake. Ted also enjoyed golfing with the children when they visited, especially Bob Swanson. Ted and Bob always had a little wager on the 17th hole, which is a 185 yard par 3 with an elevated green. It's the hardest par 3 on the course. Ted and Margaret's children and grandchildren still enjoy this nice golf course whenever they're in the area.

Ted and Margaret had a nice social life at the lake. They sometimes drove over to Clarissa and visited old friends and also socialized with many of their long-time neighbors at the lake. The first cabin to the east was owned by Dr. Lewis from Henning. He didn't know much about boats or fishing so Ted sometimes took him out. Next door was a cabin owned by Ralph Kimber, who later sold to Ruth Walden, a former schoolteacher from Minneapolis. Ruth took Margaret grocery shopping or to get her hair fixed after Ted died. Further to the east was a little resort called Minnehaha. When they came to visit, Ted and Margaret's grandchildren walked down there to buy candy.

The first cabin to the west was owned by Clint Murphy. This is where Ted and Margaret's children and their families often stayed when they came up to the lake on vacation. Next to

Minneha Resort at Battle Lake

the Murphy cabin was a lot owned by Joe Johnson. Joe was sort of an odd guy: nobody knew much about him. He worked at the meat market in Clarissa for many years and then built a cement "cave" at the lake. It was about 10 x 12 feet and had a vent and stove pipe sticking out of the top. Joe made choke cherry wine and the Wheeler and Murphy boys often went over to his place, drank his wine, and listened to his stories.

The next lot was originally owned by Reno Lundquist and stood empty for many years. Adjacent to it was a large home owned by Maurie and Lil Carlton, who were close friends of Ted and Margaret's. They owned and operated the former Wheeler's Inn restaurant and hotel in Clarissa for many years. Maurie died in the late 1950s and Lil eventually was remarried to Wilbur Tonsager. Wilbur died in 1987, but Lil, who is now in her mid-80s, still lives at the lake all year round.

Further down the road Lloyd and Maybelle Wheeler bought a cabin, which also included a guest cabin, next to the Sunset Beach resort. (It wasn't their first cabin at the lake. Originally they had a little brooder house next to Ted and Margaret's place.) For many years Bert Wheeler and his wife Dee lived in their guest cabin during the summer and in Florida during the winter. Dee died in 1988 and Bert, now 85, is at the Bethany Nursing Home in Alexandria.

Lloyd and Maybelle's first cabin at Battle Lake

It's approximately 500 miles from Grand Island, Nebraska, to Battle Lake, and Ted and Margaret always drove straight through without stopping some time in early May. The Saturday closest to May 16th is "opening day" for walleye fishing in Minnesota (a very big day!) and Ted wanted to make sure he was there for the opening. When they left the lake in the fall, the boat, shore station, and dock were pulled out of the water; the water system was drained and blown out with an air compressor so the pipes wouldn't freeze; and the windows and furniture were covered. Of course, in the spring Ted and Margaret had to reverse all these things, but they always seemed harder to do in the fall.

When members of the Wheeler family see the movie "On Golden Pond" (which starred Henry Fonda and Katharine Hepburn), they often think of Ted and Margaret at Battle Lake. Many things were very similar. The couple in the movie came to the lake every summer, they had a big wooden motorboat, there were loons on the lake, and sometime during the summer their kids (Jane Fonda) and grandkids came to visit them. More important, however, was the depiction of two strong personalities and the special relationship they enjoyed.

Ted and Margaret Wheeler at Battle Lake

OUR MEMORIES *of* BATTLE LAKE

The name "Battle Lake" strikes a chord of nostalgia within each of us. We recall making the drive to Minnesota every year and spending leisurely weeks fishing, water skiing, playing cards, and spending time with our grandparents, aunts and uncles, and cousins. We reflect fondly on those cherished memories of summers at the lake, times when we could step away from the hustle of work and school and simply spend time together with family. Following is a collection of our thoughts, compiled in 2017.

Sue: We traveled there every year when I was a child. Sometimes our parents told us we could ask an additional friend along on vacation to the lake. It was a long two-day drive and we would be so excited to finally be there. The lake was right outside the back door. I remember fishing with Dad and Grandpa Wheeler, hanging our feet over the dock and letting the minnows kiss them. Grandma taught us how to knit there. We would capture turtles and paint their shells. All my mother's family, the Murphys, had a cabin next to Grandpa and Grandma Wheeler's cabin. It was where we all learned how to water ski and fish.

Shirley: We would take vacations to Minnesota. My folks had a cabin at Battle Lake. I remember eating a lot of fish. My dad would take anybody out fishing that wanted to go. Mom had to clean the fish, and then she would fry them in butter. I fished a little. My dad would take us to water ski. I just tried that once and didn't want my father to dump me off if he turned the boat real fast.

Byron: We just traveled back and forth to Minnesota, just went one place for the summer. One time I blew up a whole bunch of firecrackers in the car with my cousin. We're still grounded from that experience. I was not hurt, but I still can't hear very well.

Debbie: Before they sold it, my kids and I would go there every summer to visit Grandma and Grandpa. I remember fishing with Grandpa for sunfish as well as swimming in the lake. Uncle Bert taking a bath in the lake was fun to watch. We played a lot of cards. We played in a chicken coop renovated into a little one room cabin. It was fun to play in, and I guess I got to sleep in it a couple times. They had a big wood boat, and I remember learning to water ski.

Sarah: Yes, we went there every summer! I was always so excited to go, and the drive seemed to take forever! We would stop in Alexandria and get groceries, and we stayed in the cabin next to Grandma and Grandpa's. I remember playing on the big inner tubes, the dock, the boathouse, especially fishing, and cleaning sunfish, playing cards, and walking the shore to Minnehaha to buy candy and play the pinball machine.

Becky: Playing games are big with Wheelers. Grandma and Grandpa would slip us a $5 bill and we'd go to Minnehaha to make choices for treats. All the grandkids loved going there. Grandpa Wheeler had a dog named Heidi who loved riding in the boat. Grandpa taught us how to fish with leeches to catch walleye. Grandma would fix them up and make cucumber salad—that went well with sunfish.

Jeni: I loved going to Battle Lake. We usually only went once a year in the summer. Grandma Wheeler's house always smelled like mothballs. Whether it was the house in Battle Lake or in Grand Island, she would put mothballs out when they would be gone for long periods of time. I remember playing cards and going fishing and Grandma frying up the fish. We fished a lot, caught sunfish.

Pam: A trip to Battle Lake took two days of driving. I loved the lake. My other grandfather, Grandpa Murphy (my mom's father), and my Grandpa Wheeler were best friends and they had cabins next to each other. When we went to Battle Lake, it really was wonderful. I learned how to water ski there. I remember catching frogs for Grandpa and boating and playing in the water. We just had a good time.

Steve: Grandpa Ted and Grandma Margaret had a cabin on Battle Lake, and we all went up there and spent a week or two in the summer fishing with Grandpa Ted for sunfish. It was like a rite of passage in the family. He would be out lowering the boat in the early morning, already halfway through a cigar. That's an epic picture of summers with Grandpa. Talk about influence . . . those visits to the lake and being on the water had a big influence on me, on all of us.

Mary Kay: I remember our immediate family would go to Battle Lake for two weeks in the summer. My Grandma and Grandpa Wheeler had a home there, and my Grandpa Murphy also did. Minnesota is just the neatest state. We just didn't go to the cabin and stay; we traveled around the area. Later on, when my parents retired, they bought a home on East Battle Lake. My brothers and sisters and our families went to their place in August, usually for the Watermelon Days festival. Every little town in Minnesota has games for kids and adults like Bingo and parades. The little churches have dinner they sell to people.

Mike: Every summer we would go up for a few weeks. I remember just fishing with Grandpa and going out every once in awhile and golfing with Dad and Grandpa. The only time I ever golfed with Grandpa was in Minnesota. I don't remember any scores. He was always hitting it right down the middle. My father could hit the golf ball a long way, but it was in the trees quite a bit.

Bill: When I was young, we would go to Minnesota in the summer and visit my grandparents at Battle Lake, usually in August. We would spend a week there—that meant lots of playing cards. My grandmother loved to play Sputnik, and my grandfather and I played Gin. My grandfather took me fishing for sunfish. Sometimes we were up at the crack of dawn. My grandparents had a very nice place, which they had for many years. One of the things I thought was so cool was my grandfather had an old wooden speedboat. He kept it in a boathouse on shore and let it down in the water on little train tracks. That was always kind of a dramatic moment when it was coming out of the boathouse.

Buzz: That's a special place. That's where my grandfather was, and we'd go fishing for sunfish. He'd take us out in the boat, and we'd come back and clean the fish, bury the remains on the beach, and my grandmother would cook the fish. My grandparents had a nice place. That was my original escape place. Vacation central. That was where our grandparents were, so it was a special place. Even after Sheila and I were married, we would go to Battle Lake. My mom and dad had a place down from my grandparents. The thing with the Wheeler family is we always need a place by the lake or water. My sister and brother and I bought the place from my folks, but wound up being so far away.

Connie: We took family vacations every year to Minnesota. That was a tradition, and we loved it. We got to see the other side of the family, too. That was the best vacation ever. I've been able to take my mom and my Aunt Bev up for one of their Clarissa high school reunions. Just last year, my sister and her children and I drove Mom back up to Minnesota. Those are neat memories, especially seeing the house where Mom lived and Grandma and Grandpa lived.

Mark: We took about every family vacation in the summer to Minnesota. It was always enjoyable, and there are lots of memories getting up early to go walleye fishing with Grandpa Wheeler. Later in the day, we would go sunfish fishing. I remember cleaning the fish. On the other hand, after a while, I kind of wondered if we could take a vacation someplace else.

Lori: Those were the best times. We would go up there every summer, and Grandpa taught all us kids to fish. But you had to clean 'em if you wanted to eat 'em. We had to put the worm on the hook, and we would catch hundreds of sunfish. He had a sauna in his boathouse. When you're a kid, that's different. We would get all hot in the sauna and then jump in the cold Minnesota lake. Anytime the family would get together they played cards, and I hate cards to this day. I couldn't count the cards, and my dad would get mad. My mom can still play cards—that's something that they taught her.

NEBRASKA

Wheeler Migration

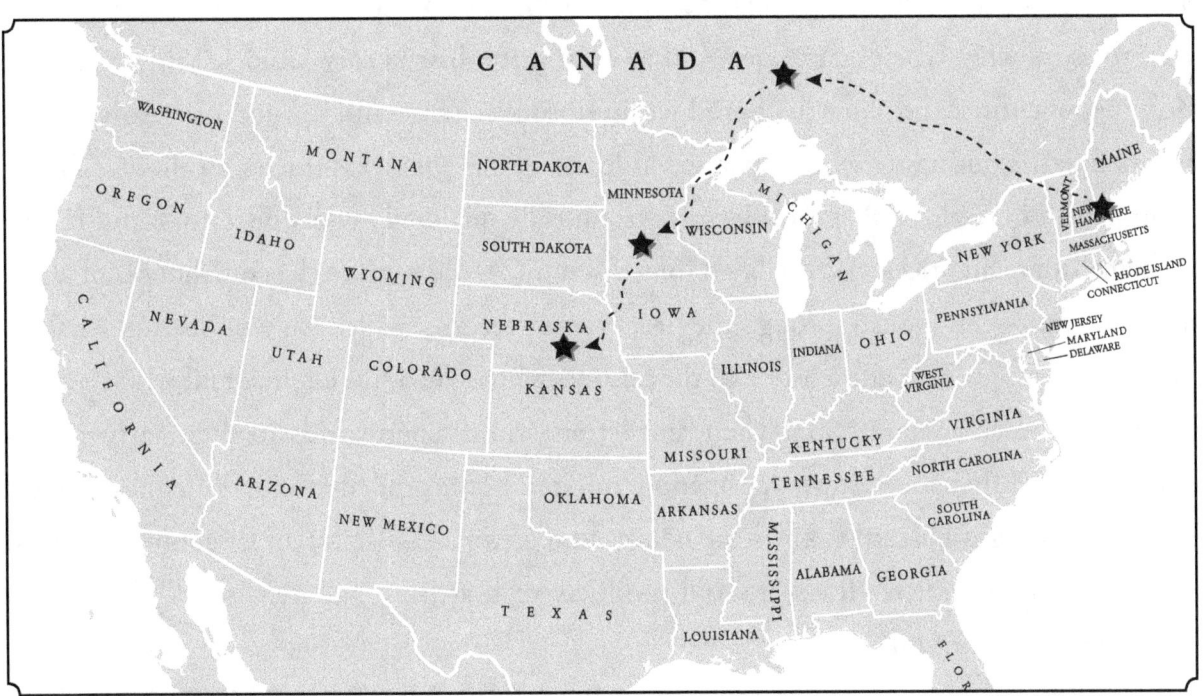

Wheeler Migration 1600–1955

In the early fall of 1954, while working at the garage, Ted and Lloyd began to notice that many of their customers were acting strange. They brought their cars in for a tune up but then told the mechanic to "just put the old spark plugs in again." After this happened a couple of times one customer admitted to Lloyd that he could buy spark plugs much cheaper from a Big Bear store in St. Cloud. The price was almost the same price that the garage paid for plugs from its wholesaler, or jobber. Ted and Lloyd asked their jobber, Mac Matheisen, what was going on. Mac explained that some retailers had joined together and were buying certain products direct from the manufacturer. Ted became very interested and called the owner of the Big Bear store, a man named Orville Peterson. Orville suggested that Ted talk to Morey Stone, who owned A&T Supply in Moorehead, Minnesota. Morey and Ted hit it off right away because they both loved to fish. Morey then explained about M.W. ("Bob") Kiesau, Mid-States Distributing Company and the farm store business.

In the 1940s, Bob Kiesau, who lived in Grand Forks, North Dakota, worked as an automotive jobber. In the late 1940s, automotive manufacturers began selling directly to dealers and oil companies began selling directly to service station operators. This didn't leave much business for the automotive jobber and Bob struggled to make a living. Then, while driving back to North Dakota from a Florida vacation in 1950, he got an idea. Manufacturers imposed strict rules on what type of customers and at what price distributors could sell their products. Most manufacturers did allow their products to be sold at a discount to "fleet operators," which were defined as businesses which operated at least five gas engines, vehicles, or pieces of heavy equipment. Bob realized that most farmers technically qualified as fleet operators, and instead of paying full retail prices they qualified for a discount. So he went to the courthouses of all the nearby counties and looked through the property tax records, which were public information. From these records he made a list of all the farmers who owned five engines and who therefore qualified for fleet discounts. Bob then sent letters and discount cards to these farmers. The letter explained that a new store was opening in Grand Forks called Home of Economy and if the farmer brought his card to the store he would receive a 25-30 percent discount from retail prices on many products. The store sold products such as tires, batteries, spark plugs, tools, antifreeze, and motor oil.

The store became successful almost immediately. Of course, today the word "discount" has lost all meaning in retailing. All but the most exclusive stores claim to sell their products at a discount. But at the time this was a radical concept, and in some people's minds (mainly competitors), almost unethical. One of Bob's problems was, with one store, he didn't generate enough volume to entice many manufacturers to sell to him. He realized that if he helped others start stores, together they would produce the necessary volume. Morey Stone and Bill and Harold Bomgaars soon started stores and experienced success as well. Harold, whose family now operates 11 farm stores, later wrote about his first store in Sioux City, Iowa:

> I can remember on one real cool afternoon in early October, I think it was the 1st of October, we did over $3,000 that day. We had never, ever done $3,000 a day in our lives, and we were just amazed. And so thrilled. We sold a tremendous amount of anti-freeze that day. And I can remember we had to haul every case of it out of the basement because we had them stored downstairs. We only had a 25 x 150 ft. operation in those days and had a machine shop in the back of it.

By late 1953, the various store owners decided to formally organize and Mid-States Distributing Company was created. The members often met and exchanged ideas about advertising, store layout, fixtures, compensation of employees, insurance, store locations, and many other issues. One of Bob Kiesau's ideas was the two price system. For example, the price tag on a piece of merchandise looked like this:

```
List      $ .99
          7697
```

When customers came into the store with their discount cards, he explained that they were entitled to the coded price between the sevens. All the Mid-States members copied this system. Techniques like this and the discount card sent a powerful message to customers about the value they were receiving.

Today, there are 62 members of Mid-States who together own over 450 stores. Bob Kiesau died in March 1984 after a long illness. His wife Jean is still operating five Home of Economy stores in North Dakota.

When Morey Stone explained the concept to Ted, there were farm stores in the Dakotas and Minnesota. Ted was very enthusiastic about the concept and shared the information with Clint Murphy and Mac Mathiesen. They decided to form a partnership and opened a store in

An early Mid-States meeting. From left to right: Ted Wheeler, Harold Bomgaars, Claude Blain, Morey Stone, Dan Dean, Cliff Melander, Bob Kiesau (standing) and Orville Peterson

Columbus, Nebraska, in March 1955. The store was named M&W Wholesale Supply Co. and it was located at 1254 28th Avenue. Although there are conflicting accounts, it appears that Mathiesen moved to Columbus to run the store. The store lost over $1,800 in March but, in a letter to Ted, Mac wrote that the business was off to a strong start:

Dear Ted;

I suppose it is about time I dropped you a line to let you know how much money you are losing. This may sound bad to you, but in consideration of the fact we have only been open a month, it looks pretty good. . . . Considering the expense we had for the start, I think we may fare out a lot better than we expected. . . .

The results in the Columbus store were very encouraging and Ted decided to sell the garage and open another store with Lloyd. The family traveled to Grand Island, Nebraska, met with members of the local Chamber of Commerce, and looked for a site for the store. Margaret remembered how nice everyone was and the positive reception they received. The city manager gave them a tour of Grand Island and the Chamber of Commerce recommended a building at 718 Front Street, which was owned by Casper Meyers. The building had about 4,000 square feet of space and was located directly across the street from some concrete grain elevators owned by Nebraska Consolidated Mills, which was later acquired by the Peavey Company. It is an interesting coincidence that 21 years after that first store opened, Peavey would also acquire Wheeler's stores.

A recent photo of the Front Street building, which was the site of the original Wheeler's store in Grand Island, Nebraska

In 1955, Grand Island had a population of approximately 24,000 and was the third largest city in the state, a distinction that is still true today (except for five or six Saturdays each fall). The name of the town seems odd, given its location in the central plains, which were once described as "the great American desert." There was an island once, though, in the middle of the Platte River, which runs about 10 miles south of Grand Island. In the nineteenth century French fur traders, paddling up the Platte on their way to the Rocky Mountains, named it "Le Grande Isle." Sometime later the Platte shifted its course and the island disappeared, but the name stuck. When German immigrants later settled the town, they called it Grand Island. Traces of the town's German heritage can still be seen today. There are a lot of blonde heads and a lot of German surnames in the phone book. The Liederkranz and the Platte-Deutsche, old German social clubs, have survived, although you don't have to be of German heritage to join them. A long time ago, maybe longer than anyone can remember, the townspeople stopped thinking of themselves as Germans, or as the descendants of Germans. Instead they became Nebraskans, and Americans, and that's what Grand Island really is: an All-American town in the middle of farm country.

The Nebraska economy is based on agriculture. This has always been true, and even though there has been a slow diversification into other economic activity, it is likely to remain true for the foreseeable future. Therefore, the farmers (and cattlemen) are responsible for most of the commerce in the state. Today, many people think of farmers as being poor, but the reality is that in many parts of Nebraska, certain farmers and cattlemen are the wealthiest people in the area. It has been said (and may have actually been true in the 1970s when land prices were high) that the average Nebraska farmer was a millionaire on paper. In hindsight, given these facts, it seems like a very good idea to open a discount store which targeted the people responsible for most of the economic activity in the area, and who were also very price sensitive. At the time however, there were a lot of skeptics.

In the last part of June 1955, Ted, Margaret, Lloyd, Maybelle, six-year-old Bruce, and Lloyd and Maybelle's two-week-old baby Byron moved to Grand Island. It was hot, much hotter than Minnesota, and the houses they moved into didn't have any air conditioning. After getting settled, Ted and Lloyd began to convert the Front Street building into a store. They painted the inside, and had a local carpenter build fixtures out of plywood. The carpenter also built a checkout counter up front and a wall near the back of the store to give Ted and Lloyd a place to receive merchandise from the freight companies. They also bought a cash register, and the man who sold it to them later told Lloyd he made certain he was paid in cash because he didn't think the store would last a year.

In order to figure out what merchandise to order, they looked at the results from the store in Columbus. They bought tires, batteries, spark plugs, fan belts, anti-freeze, motor oil, greases, paint, chains, twine, rope, air compressors, electric motors, and all kinds of tools. The total inventory cost less than $14,000, so they arranged it to make it look like there was a lot more. They also chose a name for the store: Wheeler's Farm Supply. It doesn't seem very original (given Wheeler's Inn and Wheeler's Sales & Service), but it certainly was consistent.

One morning Ted decided to open a bank account for the store and said to Lloyd that one bank was as good as another. Lloyd remembers that the Overland National Bank had a parking space in front and so that's where they opened the account. The bank also recommended an outside accountant named E.B. Foster. Working with Foster was a young man named Bernie Corrigan. Bernie eventually took over Foster's business and later joined Wheeler's.

Prior to the opening, Margaret and Lloyd visited all the county seats in the area. Besides Grand Island these included Aurora, Broken Bow, Central City, Hastings, Loup City, and St. Paul. They looked through the property tax statements from the prior year and compiled a mailing list of all the farmers who had five or more engines. Bob Albee of Albee Printing printed up the discount cards and the letter for the first mailing. It was decided to put the discount cards in plastic so that the customer might place a little more importance to them. Twenty years later, some farmers were still carrying these cards in their wallets. The cards and letters were then placed in envelopes which were personally addressed by hand. They were mailed in early August.

The store was now ready to open. When the first customers walked in on August 15, 1955, the store must have seemed a little amateurish with its concrete floors and homemade fixtures and signs. But there may have been another message as well. Think of the successful warehouse club stores of today with their membership cards, concrete floors, and cheap fixtures. The customer thinks he is getting a great price because it's obvious that overhead costs have been kept to a minimum. Though it was hardly by choice, one could say that in some ways Wheeler's Farm Supply was ahead of its time.

The first day the store took in over $500. Everyone was happy with the sales, but they were also happy with the reaction from customers. In any business it's important to listen to the customers and find out what their needs are. The store always had a pot of coffee on for its customers so that Ted and Lloyd could sit down and get to know them. (Free coffee became a standard fixture in the stores for many years.)

One product that customers asked for immediately were siphon tubes. Ted and Lloyd had never even heard of a siphon tube, but they soon learned that it was a curved piece of aluminum pipe which siphons irrigation water out of the main ditch to each row of corn. They quickly found a place to buy siphon tubes and got them into the store as soon as possible. Over the years, Wheeler's sold an enormous number of siphon tubes. Ted and Lloyd were learning that farming and ranching in Nebraska were a lot different than in Minnesota.

It was also important to have the right price on certain key products, because the customer may judge the entire store based on how one or two items were priced. In the 1950s, one of those key items was Champion Spark Plugs. The list price, which everyone paid, was 85 cents

Wheeler's Farm Supply
"Lloyd and Ted" Wheeler

FARM SUPPLIES AT WHOLESALE

FREE CUSTOMER PARKING

718 WEST FRONT STREET

GRAND ISLAND, NEBRASKA

Tires

Batteries

Spark Plugs

Tractor Sleeves

Chains

Chain Saws

Gaskets

Electrical Appliances

Anti-Freeze

Twine

Rope

Motor Oil

Greases

Grease Equipment

Weed Spray

Fan Belts

Plastic Pipe

Lawn Mowers

Paint

Tools

Brake Shoes

Ignition

Garden Hose

Air Compressors

Electric Motors

    Fleet owners all over the country are benefiting by large discounts their standing brings them. Until a few years ago these Fleet discounts were limited to large companies operating five or more trucks or autos.

    Now in the northwest there are already 35 Fleet Supply stores who are extending Fleet Owners Discounts to farmers who qualify. Thousands of farmers have been issued similar Fleet owner discount cards because they operate five or more autos, trucks and tractors or gas engines. They are saving 25% to 30% on things they buy.

    We have opened a Farmers Wholesale Store in the Casper Meyer Building across the street from the Nebraska Consolidated Mills Company. We are directly above the Eddy Street underpass in the same building as Willman's Grocery. There is plenty of customer parking space.

    We carry a complete line of nationally advertised products, those you have been buying for years. We are not a chain store but we do carry and offer you substantial discounts on many farm items such as tools, electric motors, house and barn paint, baler twine, tarpaulin, and air compressors. We have Armstrong car, truck and tractor tires which carry a lifetime unconditional guarantee.

    As records show you operate five or more gasoline powered units, we have prepared this Fleet Discount Card in your name. This card entitles you to a discount on every item we sell, but of course, you must present it at the time of your purchase. The average discount runs 30%. Some items such as oil filters carry a discount of 50%, some items discounted at only 15%, but on the average your discount will be about 30% below the prices you would otherwise pay.

    Here are examples of your savings...Champion Spark Plugs 85c list—wholesale 53c... D 24 Dura-Start battery $20.30 list—wholesale $14.89. Baler twine $6.60 per bale.

    PUT THIS FLEET DISCOUNT CARD IN YOUR WALLET NOW and the next time you are in Grand Island come in and look over the many articles you regularly use that you now can buy wholesale. Free customer parking is available. We are open from 7 a.m. to 6 p.m.

Yours very truly,

Lloyd and Ted Wheeler

WHEELER'S FARM SUPPLY

The original letter that was mailed to farmers for the opening on August 15, 1955, of the Wheeler's Farm Supply store in Grand Island, Nebraska

per plug. Wheeler's Farm Supply sold them for 53 cents per plug and advertised them for that price in its original mailer. Half of the customers that walked in the store wanted to see those Champion Spark Plugs for 53 cents. Some even asked if the plugs were factory seconds. Lloyd believes that Champion Spark Plugs contributed more to the success of the farm store concept than any other single product.

Around the first of October the store had its first $1,000 day, and the sales kept increasing. Many of the original customers told their friends and neighbors about the store. They then came in and applied for their own discount card. Other key factors for the sales growth were additional inventory and advertising. The store's first mailer was sent in October.

The original mailer for the Wheeler's Farm Supply store in Grand Island

Wheeler's Farm Supply remained pretty much a family business for a number of years. The store didn't hire its first outside full-time employee until June of 1956. Margaret worked at the store, both in the office and on the floor. Maybelle was taking care of her two boys but also came down to the store when needed. In 1959, Lloyd and Maybelle added a daughter, Deborah, to their family.

Other members of the Wheeler family began to get involved in the operation. In 1956, Bob and Shirley Swanson, along with their daughter Connie, age four, and a new baby boy, Steve, moved from Columbus, Nebraska, to Grand Island. Bob worked in the Grand Island store for about a year before starting a store in North Platte, Nebraska, in 1957. When Bob and Shirley bought a house in North Platte, Ted strongly recommended air conditioning. Shirley remembers, "We were so surprised as Dad didn't usually say what to do." Bob and Shirley had two more children while in North Platte: Mike was born in 1958 and Sarah was born in 1963.

After Jim Wheeler was discharged from the Marine Corps in 1954, he bought a bulldozer and started a land clearing business in North Carolina. While in North Carolina, Jim and Mona had three daughters: Mary Kay was born in 1952 at Camp LeJeune; and Sue and Pam were born in New Bern in 1956 and 1957, respectively. In 1958, the family came to Nebraska and Jim worked with Bob Swanson for a year at the store in North Platte. He then opened a store in Lexington, Nebraska, in 1959. Jim would later say that his favorite day of the year was Christmas Eve: "People who came into the store didn't want to shop, they wanted to buy." A son, Bill, was born in Lexington in 1961.

Pete and Beverly Swanson, along with their one year old son Mark, came to Grand Island from St. Cloud, Minnesota, in 1958. Pete worked in the Grand Island store for a year and then started a store in Broken Bow, Nebraska, in 1959. Pete, who was 25 at the time, later wrote:

"My experience in starting and running a store was nil. I had never been on my own to manage but Ted and Margaret's patience and faith in me was a real motivation. While getting the store organized, I slept and lived at the store until Bev and I found a home in Broken Bow . . . I only hope I conveyed to Ted and Margaret my gratitude and appreciation for giving me the opportunity to be part of the stores. They always treated me as a son and I thought the world of them."

Pete and Beverly later had three daughters: Lori was born in Grand Island in 1959; Becky in Broken Bow in 1960; and Jeni back in Grand Island in 1970.

Besides raising their young children, all of the wives worked in the stores. They helped during the busy seasons (especially Christmas), when there were store openings, when inventory was counted, and also obtained names from county courthouses for the mailing list. Nobody can remember any of them ever getting paid for this work. Eventually, all but a few of their children (and some of their children's spouses) spent some time working in the stores.

Ted and Margaret and their four children were back together. Although various members of the family lived in different towns in Nebraska, they saw each other often, either through the business or through holiday get-togethers. Practically every Thanksgiving and Christmas, the families of the four children came to Ted and Margaret's house in Grand Island. There were big meals, football games on television (the University of Nebraska often played its rival, Oklahoma, on Thanksgiving Day), and an increasing number of children to keep an eye on. At Christmas, Ted and Margaret bought everyone a present, and sometime during the afternoon Santa stopped by and handed them out. Originally, Ted was Santa Claus but he soon found someone else to play the part. For many years, each grandkid also received a $50 U.S. Savings Bond. These holiday gatherings were the family's main rituals and because of the presents, the smell of turkey in the oven, the chance to play with their cousins, and the grandparents who were always so happy to see them, they created a lot of pleasant memories for each grandkid.

MEMORIES of OUR GRANDPARENTS: TED AND MARGARET WHEELER

We each have fond recollections about Grandma and Grandpa Wheeler. Some of us lived near them and saw them frequently, while others only spent time with them on occasion. Regardless, we all recognize the significant impact that they made on our lives. Grandma and Grandpa were exceptional folks who shaped the very core of the family. We look up to them as examples of just how far a little dreaming and a lot of hard work can take you in this country. We're thankful for the example they set; we each, in our own way, are trying to carry their legacy forward through our dedication and service to those around us. Following is a collection of our thoughts, compiled in 2017.

Lori: Before they started the store and raising their kids, they had a restaurant. Grandpa ran an auto repair place and then a skating rink on the nights and weekends. He seemed to enjoy working. That's even true with me—I get enjoyment from work. I think that's just the way it was spending time with them. Anytime we did something together, it was work.

Sue: They would tell us stories about our father getting into trouble when he was bad, which are always fun for children to hear. I remember hearing that the day they got married they then went and picked corn in the field the same day. That impressed me. They were hardworking people.

Becky: Grandma was busy, busy, busy. She would make candles or play cards with us—she always had something going on that made it a lot of fun to go over to her house. Grandpa Wheeler was quiet, but even though he was quiet, having an activity like fishing makes the bonds between generations so special. It was so easy to fish there at Battle Lake with him.

Jeni: My grandma loved watching *Dallas* and *Falcon Crest*. It was neat as a pin there. If she didn't agree with you, she made a sound like "aaahhh." The older she got, she always had a frog in her throat. She had peanut butter toast with coffee in the morning. Grandma Wheeler sewed things like pillows and embroidered shirts. She was always crafty with things. One year she took a bunch of costume jewelry and made a Christmas tree with the costume jewelry, outlined it with lights, and framed it. She was just such a good egg.

My grandpa died when I was in fifth or sixth grade. He had his heart attack at our house, something I will never forget. Grandpa didn't always say a lot, but you knew he loved you. He loved his yard. They had a wiener dog named Heidi, who they used to give ice cream to before they went to bed. At their house, there was a little room off the kitchen with a little red chair and a desk. I would go in and color in there. After Grandpa died and Grandma made the decision to sell the house on Anna Street, they had a garage sale. Aunt Shirl and Mom and the uncles helped her out. Everyone always made sure that Grandma was taken care of. They were a good group of people.

Debbie: What I remember about my grandfather was him fishing and cigar smoking. Both my dad and grandpa napped after lunch and dinner. They were napping kind of guys. Once we ate, all the kids would go out to a movie, probably 12-15 grandkids. They always had a dachshund—and fed it ice cream every night.

We had big family gatherings where we would gather at Grandma and Grandpa's for Thanksgiving and Christmas. The ladies always had a great big bucket of frozen daiquiris.

Buzz: I can remember my grandmother cooking or baking for all the members of the family. She made sure everybody felt comfortable and appreciated. There was always room for everybody at Grandma's table. They were salt-of-the-earth people who worked very, very hard. In their later years, I remember the care that my folks gave them in making sure their last years were comfortable. That was something they were taught, and then I was able to do that with my parents. The neat thing to see is that move from one generation to another, the bestowing of honor on the generation before.

Bill: They both passed away when I was still pretty young. I think I have a much better appreciation for their lives and what they did after I helped my Uncle Lloyd write the first Wheeler's book. That gave me a great understanding for their lives and what they're like. They went through a lot of struggle and came from nothing. They built a livelihood for their families and set us on a different path.

Sarah: I remember Grandpa Wheeler smoking his pipe and Grandma in her garden at Battle Lake. I remember helping with the green beans, and learning how to scale the fish after we caught them. Grandpa would routinely slip a $5 in our hands! I loved being in Grandma's bathroom with her hair brushes and mirror. She had long hair for quite awhile.

Shirley: Mom was a good cook. She could make anything.

Becky: I remember being with Grandpa at a gas station. He would pump his own gas because it was a penny cheaper.

Connie: I still have that insurance that they gave each of the grandchildren. Other times they gave us money, and it went in the bank right away. Grandma always fed us on little plates—not a whole lot of food, little food but good food. Grandpa fell asleep in his chair after dinner. They had a Cuckoo clock. I remember sleeping down in the basement and they had a picture of a wolf. The famous wolf picture gave me nightmares. Grandma didn't drive, but Grandpa picked her up and would take her to get her hair done. I do have an old humpback chest that has LH Wheeler on top of it.

That is a special treasure. I have the grandfather clock that their children gave to them on their 50th wedding anniversary.

Mary Kay: I remember funny little things. My grandmother was a perfectionist, and it was very important to her to have a clean, clean home and be a good cook. She liked having her family around. My grandpa was kind of like a teddy bear. My grandmother never drove, so later on after they moved to Nebraska, he would take her wherever she needed to go. He would take her to her Friday hair appointment and to the doctor – he was always more than happy to drive her wherever she needed to go. He would usually go home for lunch, and after lunch take a 15-minute nap on the couch in the family room, then pop up and go play cards or go do what he was going to do. He was a great guy and had a wonderful laugh that he passed down to his children.

They always made Christmas dinner. When we were young, we always went to Grandma and Grandpa's for Christmas Day. Grandpa loved to hunt, and he and my husband, when we were first married, often went deer hunting together. A couple of times, they left real early in the morning before dawn. Then they would come to our house, and I would fix them breakfast. That's a special memory.

Mark: Grandpa Wheeler worked a lot, so we would just see him on special occasions. I remember him and his Mercedes and the cigars. I didn't really get a feel for him until I was in my 20s and we were in California, and then he wasn't with us much longer. We saw quite a bit of Grandma. Mom would take us over there, and she always liked to serve us little glasses of 7 Up and maybe a cracker or two. She seemed a bit stern and serious, but she cared about you.

Pam: My grandparents were good people, honest people, hardworking people, but I wasn't around them a huge amount. Other cousins were around them a lot more. I loved them, but I wasn't really close to them. I guess one time they came and babysat. I want to be there a lot as a grandparent and spend lots of time with my grandchildren. It wasn't really a relationship like that with my grandparents. They were kind and hardworking.

If you had another chance to speak to your grandparents, what would you say to them?

Sue: I'd say, "Thank you. You successfully raised a family and had a positive influence on all of the grandchildren."

Jeni: "Thank you. You provided me with a lot of good memories."

Becky: When Grandma Wheeler died, I remember being extra sad because we were at the stage where it was an adult friendship where I could call and share. I would love to tell them how much I admire them. As I read the book, I just realize the determination that they had. They worked so hard during hard times, and they raised four kids who could get along together. It still simply amazes me. I would love to hear their stories. How did they manage that?

Connie: I love them. They were sharing. I appreciated how they helped me grow. I would just thank them. I wish I could hug them again.

Buzz: "Thank You." I think there's not a day that goes by that I don't reach out and remember something that my grandfather or my mom and dad taught me.

Mary Kay: I'd like for them to know Sarah and thank them for the good start in life that they gave to us. My grandpa passed away before she was born. Sarah was just a toddler when my grandmother passed away.

Sarah: I would tell them they had an amazing life, raising four kids and being involved in all the businesses, especially Wheelers, and it was just really cool how much fun they had, too! I would give them a really tight hug and tell them I loved them.

Mark: "Thank you." For the amount that they instilled achieving goals. It's not like I'm driven in the way Jim and Lloyd and Grandpa seemed to be, but I wanted to be successful.

Byron: How'd you find your drive? In retrospect, they kind of liked making things happen.

Pam: I think it was a great legacy. They were great people. I'm happy my dad was who he was because of the way he was raised, both the good and the bad. I think his parents were really strict. I would say, "Thanks. It was great. You did a great job."

Wheeler's Farm Supply now began to grow and change more dramatically. New stores were opened or acquired, existing stores were moved to better and larger locations, a warehouse and trucking distribution system was developed, the product lines offered became broader, computer systems were installed, and people outside the family were hired for key positions in the company. As almost anyone who has ever worked at a fast growing, successful company will tell you, it was a fun time to be at Wheeler's.

The first store that was not managed by a family member was opened in Kearney, Nebraska, in 1960. Bob Lewis was the manager and the Kearney store did at least as well, and often better, than the other stores. Six more new stores were opened by 1968, when the company did its first acquisition. Six stores were acquired from Melvin Lonowski: three were in eastern Nebraska, two in Iowa, and one in Kansas. In 1973, four stores in the Nebraska panhandle and Wyoming were acquired from Kenneth Pickard and, in 1974, the Fort Collins, Colorado,

Christmas, 1958. From left to right: back row, Pete Swanson, Beverly (Wheeler) Swanson, Maybelle (Lundgren) Wheeler, Lloyd Wheeler, Mike Swanson, Shirley (Wheeler) Swanson, Steve Swanson, Bob Swanson, Mona (Murphy) Wheeler, Pam Wheeler and Jim Wheeler; front row, Mark Swanson, Bruce Wheeler, Ted Wheeler, Byron Wheeler, Margaret Wheeler, Sue Wheeler, Connie Swanson and Mary Kay Wheeler.

store was also acquired. Ken Pickard was originally a paint salesman and sold Wheeler's its first order of paint in 1955. He saw how successful the farm stores were becoming and decided to start his own store in Scottsbluff, Nebraska.

Selecting new store locations was, at best, an educated guess. Management often just chose the county seat, which was usually the largest town in the area. If there was a good building available, or at least good real estate on which a new building could be built, a store manager was selected and plans were made to get the store opened. Despite its simplicity, the system must have worked reasonably well because from 1955 to 1976 the company didn't close a single store (although stores were sometimes moved to a different location in the same town).

The Wheeler family in the mid-1960s. From left to right: back row, Byron Wheeler, Maybelle (Lundgren) Wheeler, Mark Swanson, Bruce Wheeler, Beverly (Wheeler) Swanson, Pete Swanson, Mary Kay Wheeler, Jim Wheeler, Sue Wheeler, Mona (Murphy) Wheeler, Connie Swanson, Bob Swanson, Steve Swanson; middle row, Debbie Wheeler, Lloyd Wheeler, Ted Wheeler, Margaret Wheeler, Shirley (Wheeler) Swanson and Sarah Swanson; front row, Lori Swanson, Becky Swanson, Pam Wheeler, Mike Swanson and Bill Wheeler.

Most of the new buildings were 8,000-12,000 square feet and were constructed with masonry block. Usually the local bank loaned the company the money for the building. And when the store was stocked with merchandise, it was a great opportunity to remove excess inventory from the existing stores. Often a store was moved from one building to another in the same town because of the need for a larger building, a better location, or better lease terms. The moves generally occurred over a weekend and management tried to make them fun. The first thing moved to the new store was the cash register, so business was done in both locations during the day. Everyone who owned a pickup would bring it and more were rented from local car dealers. Two people were assigned to each pickup and given an area of the store to move. They would transfer the inventory and then merchandise it in the new location. The customers never seemed to mind shopping at two stores (of course, the distance between the stores was usually small). And it gave the company an excuse to have a moving sale, and after getting settled in the new location, a Grand Opening sale.

Grand Openings were a lot of fun, especially in new towns, and would last for three or four days. Over the years, almost everyone in the Wheeler family helped at Grand Openings. There were special prices on certain items, free drawings for prizes, and free soda and hot dogs. It was always amazing how far people came to register for prices at these Grand Openings. One memorable Grand Opening was at Gothenburg, Nebraska, in 1962. Wheeler's gave away two ponies and saddles, which created a lot of excitement.

Shirley and Bob Swanson attend to the ponies at the Gothenburg, Nebraska, Grand Opening in 1962.

The night before the Grand Opening was over, there was usually a cocktail party and dinner for everyone who helped. This included employees of the store and home office, other managers in the area, and also manufacturer's representatives who had displayed and explained their products to customers. A lot of friendships developed at those celebrations still exist today.

Grand Opening
4 Big Days, Sept. 16-17-18-19

WHEELER'S FARM SUPPLY
Hwy. 30 West

Lexington, Nebraska

BIG GRAND PRIZE
No. 50 Wagon Hoist - Retail Value $99.50

Because you are a holder of one of our FLEET DISCOUNT CARDS you are cordially invited to attend the "GRAND OPENING" of our store to be held on September 16-17-18-19, 1959. There will be free coffee and doughnuts for all who attend plus many worthwhile prizes and a variety of GRAND OPENING SPECIALS.

There will also be on hand various Factory Representatives to answer any questions that you might have in their different lines, such as paint, oil filters, grease and oil and tires, and, we will have a veterinarian.

Mark these RED LETTER DAYS on your calendar and plan to come in and look over our money-saving merchandise at WHOLESALE PRICES. Don't forget the dates, September 16-17-18-19.

FREE Filter To Everyone

To induce you to try our Harvest King Oil Filters and prove to your satisfaction that we do have a superior Oil Filter, we are offering you, at absolutely no cost to you, any filter in our stock (your choice) for your old filter. Just bring us your old filter and take home a new one. This offer good only for 4 days, September 16-17-18-19.

FREE BALLOONS FOR THE KIDDIES
See Reverse Side for Additional Free Prizes

Advertisement for the Grand Opening of the Wheeler's Farm Supply store in Lexington, Nebraska, in 1959

There was also another memorable annual sale called "Peanut Days," which was held in the fall and ran for several days. Hog pans filled with peanuts were placed all over the store with signs explaining that the peanuts were free and to just throw the shells on the floor. The floors weren't swept during the sale and the piles of peanut shells were quite a sight. Another memorable Grand Opening, although for a different reason, was the opening of the new Grand Island store at the corner of Webb Road and Highway 30 in 1966. Ted and Jim were driving to the store together and, as Ted turned left into the store parking lot, they were struck by an oncoming car. The car was demolished and Ted and Jim were both taken to the hospital but neither suffered serious injuries.

By 1976, when the business was sold, there were 45 Wheeler's stores. Most of the stores were in Nebraska, but there were also stores in Iowa, Kansas, Colorado, and Wyoming, as well as three stores in Georgia. Georgia represented an attempt to expand the business outside of its existing geographic area. The stores in Georgia never did very well, at least in relation to the rest of business. Lloyd has speculated on the reasons why:

"1. By 1974 we were not using discount cards any more and maybe we lost that personal relationship with the farmer in Georgia that we enjoyed in Nebraska.
2. We may have went into too cheap of a building with our first store.
3. Maybe we never put in the right inventory.
4. Maybe we didn't spend enough money for advertising when we opened.
5. There was also a lot of absentee ownership on Georgia farms which may have been a factor."

From the beginning, one of the biggest problems in the business was keeping the proper levels of merchandise in the stores. Initially, the manufacturers shipped the company's orders via common carrier, but this sometimes took 10 days to two weeks, which was too slow. The stores experienced stockouts and it was expensive to pay common carrier rates for shipping. The company had a small warehouse on West Anna Street in Grand Island, which was used to split larger shipments down into allocations for the various stores. A 1960 Ford Cabover with a 16 foot van was used to make deliveries to the stores. But in 1962 the company purchased its first semi-tractor and trailer—a GMC V6 diesel—and L&L Distributing Company was born. The company could now call in an order to a manufacturer, a pickup date would be agreed upon, and two or three days later the merchandise would be in the stores.

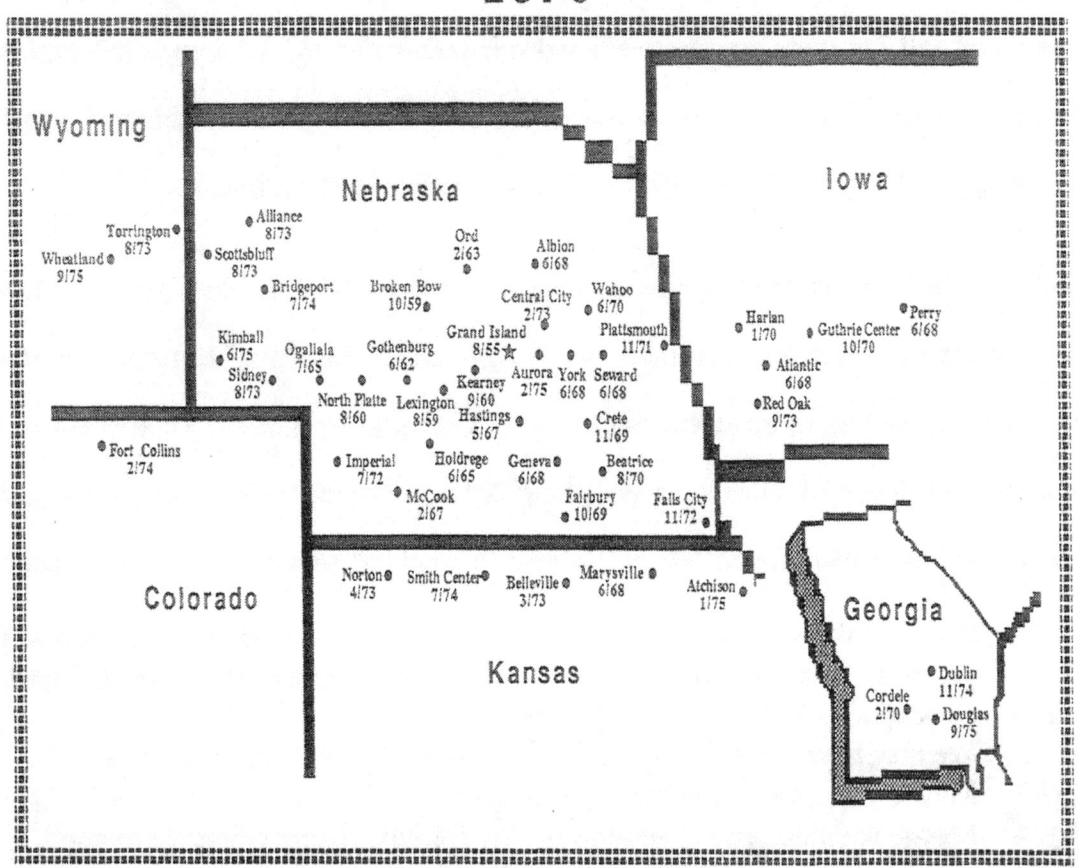

This chart shows the location of the 45 Wheeler's stores in 1976 as well as the date each store opened.

From this beginning the operation grew dramatically, A new 50,000-square-foot warehouse was built next to the store in Grand Island in 1967 and the company continued to purchase additional trucks. In order to lower the costs of the distribution system, the company did a lot of backhauling. Products such as popcorn, potatoes, and onions were hauled from Nebraska to other parts of the country. Beans were sent to the east coast of the United States from the Brown Bean Company in Morrill, Grant, and Gering, Nebraska. Honey was picked up in Grand Island, Ord, and Petersburg, Nebraska, and delivered to Lott, Ohio. And, believe it or not, the company shipped cheese from Nebraska to Wisconsin.

The men and equipment at L&L Distributing Company. From left to right: Jerry Leitchuck, Ray Morse, Morris Nitzel and Ted Wheeler. The GMC behind Ted was the company's first semi.

L&L Distributing grew quickly to support the store operations.

The merchandising strategy at Wheeler's changed very little over the years. In the beginning the concept was to supply the needs of the farmer and that really never changed, although the definition of what the farmer needed was continually being widened. The product lines listed below give some indication of the broad range of merchandise Wheeler's carried.

PRODUCT LINES
Partial List

Bailing Wire
Tires
Barbed Wire
Tee Posts
Electric Posts
Electric Wire
Cattle & Hog Panels
Field Sprayers
Field Chemicals
Power Lawn Mowers
Oil, Oil Filters & Grease
Paint & Accessories
Hand Tools
Spray Paint Equipment
Well Pumps & Pump Jacks
Hydraulic & Hi Lift Jacks
Hydraulic Cylinders, Controls
Window Fans
Bailing Twine
Wagon Gears & Boxes
Sweep Teeth
Trucks & Auto Rebuilt Engines
Brake Shoes & Water Pumps
Electric Wire, Parts & Fixtures
Lumber & Studs
Gates
Wagon Hoists
Shovels & Forks
Garden Tools
Welders & Rods
Shotgun & Rifle Shells
Fuel Tanks
Cattle & Hog Feeders
Stock Water Tanks
Animal Health Supplies
Nails & Staples
Cattle Handling Equipment

Small Electric Kitchen Appliances
Chain Saws
Air Compressors, Hose, Couplers & Tanks
Tractor Cabs & Heat Covers
Culverts
Cookies & Candy
Rope & Cable
Chicken Equipment, Feeders & Nests
Sausage & Wieners
Free Coffee
Shoes & Boots
Rubber Foot Wear
Work Clothes
Spark Plugs
Bolt & Nuts
Hydraulic Hoses & Couplers
Plow Lathes & Parts
V Belts & Flat Belts
Siphon Tubes
Irrigation Dams
Irrigation Pipes
Batteries & Chargers
Anti Freeze
Mower Parts & Sickles
Cultivator Sweeps & Bolts
Work Gloves
Salt & Mineral Blocks
Electric Motors & Supplies
Pipe Fittings & Nipples
Gas & Electric Post Hole Diggers
Toys & Christmas Items
Grain Bins & Corn Cribs
Mounted Tractor Blades - 6' & 8'
Rear Mount Weed Mowers
Tool Bars
Wood Fence Posts

The inside of a typical Wheeler's store

Some of the bigger product line additions over the years were clothing, lumber, and gasoline. The company first put gas pumps outside its store in Hastings, Nebraska, in 1972. This turned out to be a terrific idea because, other than the cost of the pumps and tanks, the business didn't add any additional overhead expense. Wheeler's made it a point to have the lowest price on gas in town and this sometimes led to price wars. The gas business improved traffic and eventually became so successful that the company began to report gas sales and profits separately from store operations.

Not all product additions worked as well as the gasoline business. In the early 1970s, farmers in Nebraska were installing a lot of center pivot irrigation systems. Wheeler's felt that because of its strong relationship with farmers, this might be a good business for the company. They negotiated a good price from a manufacturer in Wisconsin, printed some sales literature, and hired a salesman to follow up on prospects. Only one system was sold, and that was to Con Schneider's family farm. The unit worked well but the business was a failure. The business required the ability to finance customers and a high level of service—two things Wheeler's didn't have.

An important part of growing a business is attracting, motivating, and retaining good people. Wheeler's had a large number of capable long time employees who were very important to the success of the business. Lloyd writes, "It seems to me that people in Nebraska know how to work and that's the way they were brought up . . . " Another important factor was the company's profit sharing plan, which was started in 1964. Both Wheeler's and the employee could

An idea that didn't work, "Wheel-O-Matic" center pivot irrigation systems

make contributions to a profit sharing trust, which was then invested in stocks and bonds. The trust experienced good growth because no taxes were paid on the investment income until the employee withdrew his share. There was also an incentive compensation plan for managers, which was based on a formula using labor costs as a percentage of sales.

Many employees were able to carry forward the entrepreneurial spirit created by the family as the business grew. In a letter to Lloyd, Con Schneider, who joined Wheeler's in 1964, wrote about his introduction to the business:

We interviewed that evening and I was impressed with the sincerity of both you and Jim and was especially excited by the growth plans that you two laid out. You were both very enthused about what you were doing and about the future of the company. I left that particular interview with a whole different attitude about the retail business . . . I went to work on Monday, Nov. 2nd (1964), at the office in GI. I never will forget my surprise when I found out I wouldn't just be sitting on my "butt" in the buying office but would be loading trucks, unloading trucks, splitting merchandise, and then, at times, driving the small truck at night. However, as I look back, I wouldn't have traded the work situation for anything. I learned a lot about the company and a lot about myself during the initial periods with Wheeler's!

The following employees all made a significant contribution to the success of Wheeler's over the years (this list was created from memory, so please accept an apology for anyone who was inadvertently excluded):

Maxine Baasch	Jim Lighthill
Delores (Dee) Brown	Stan Longmore
Bernie Corrigan	Dale Lyons
Tony Curtis	Ray Morse
Gary Dreesen	Inez Niemoth
Ron Dreesen	Morris Nitzel
Art Duensing	Harold Price
John Fiala	Wayne Rieke
Shirley Foster	Joy Ritterbush
Jo Ann Frickey	Con Schneider
Rich Fryzck	Bill Skaggs
Dale Fusselman	Don Skeen
Bob Geisler	Jack Taylor
Vince Gergen	Kersey Welty
Bob Golden	Sam Welty
Delbert Herganrader	Dick Westcott
Adolph Hildebrandt	Meridith (Mert) White
Bob Lewis	De Wayne Wicht
Jerry Leitchuck	Joe Yanken

Ted and Margaret were both very active in the business until the early 1960s, when they turned over the day-to-day decision making to their children. Ted sometimes let them know if he thought they were doing something wrong and also sometimes let them learn from their mistakes themselves. He was good at asking searching questions and enjoyed working on the floor and meeting customers. One of his greatest strengths was his ability to meet and visit with people. Later on, when the new executive offices were built on Potash Road, Ted moved into an office of his own. He got the mail every morning and then did anything else that was needed. He always wanted to make a contribution by doing something for the company.

One might assume that with so many family members in the business, there were a significant number of problems and disagreements. There were some minor issues but nothing serious. Ted and Margaret probably contributed to this atmosphere of cooperation because they always made sure they treated all their children the same. Eventually, almost all of Ted and Margaret's grandchildren, as well as many of their spouses, worked at Wheeler's. Ted and Margaret's children all stayed in the business for many years and only began leaving after the company was sold.

Jim Wheeler receiving a plaque from his brother, Lloyd Wheeler, upon Jim's retirement from the business in 1976

Lloyd J. Wheeler began the business with Ted and Margaret in 1955. He ran the store in Grand Island until the early 1960s and then moved to the offices on West Anna. Lloyd was the President of the company until his retirement in 1982. Lloyd's son Bruce ("Buzz") Wheeler also worked at Wheeler's for a number of years, eventually running the business from 1987 to 1990. Buzz now owns his own group of stores in Oregon.

James H. Wheeler joined the business in 1958, spending a year in North Platte with Bob Swanson before starting the store in Lexington in 1959. By the mid-1960s, he was supervising overall store operations. In order to increase his productivity, the company bought Jim a Cessna Skylane in 1968 and he began to fly from store to store. Jim and his family moved to Grand Island in 1975 and he retired shortly after the sale of the business in 1976. Jim's daughter Mary Kay worked at Wheeler's for a number of years. She eventually married a co-worker, Jim Tuma, and left the business. Jim Tuma is the only remaining family member who still works at the company.

Robert W. Swanson joined the business in 1956, working in the Grand Island store. In 1957, he started a store in North Platte, which he managed until 1968. Bob, Shirley and their family then moved to Grand Island, where he worked in the office until 1971. The family then moved to Atlantic, Iowa, where Bob managed the Atlantic store and was an area manager until his retirement in 1977. Bob died of a heart attack on November 5, 1978.

Peter W. Swanson joined the business in 1958, working in the Grand Island store for almost one year. In 1959, he started a store in Broken Bow, which he managed until 1968. Pete, Beverly, and their family then moved to Grand Island, where he worked in the office until his retirement in 1977.

Bob and Pete Swanson at the Ogallala, Nebraska Grand Opening in 1965

Until the late 1960s, Wheeler's was actually a group of separate corporations, one for each store, which were owned by varying combinations of family members. The structure made it very difficult to allocate expenses such as shipping, advertising, and other overhead. Bernie Corrigan came up with the idea to form a holding company and issue stock to individual members of the family in direct proportion to the value of their stock in the individual store corporations. This was the first step in the company's long term strategy to provide liquidity for its owners.

For many years the members of the Wheeler family were paid modest salaries so that the profit from the business could be reinvested in order to open more stores, buy more inventory and trucks, as well as enlarge the warehouse and offices. The Wheeler family decided that if they were going to enjoy the wealth they had created they would either have to sell the business or take it public in a stock offering. A public offering of stock required several years of audited financial statements, so in 1968 the company hired an outside accounting firm. It was also decided to bring in some outsiders for the company's board of directors. The first outside director was Orville Peterson (the man Ted Wheeler had first called in 1954 to learn about the farm store business). The second outside director was Dick Westcott, who later joined the company as Chief Operating Officer.

In 1975, it was decided to explore the sale of Wheeler's to another company. A commercial banker from one of the large Minneapolis banks was contacted and he provided the company with a list of three candidates. The first was immediately crossed off because there didn't appear to be a fit. The second was a Minneapolis-based retailer. After several meetings, it seemed clear that Wheeler's would lose much of its independence if it was acquired by this company. The third name on the list was the Peavey Company, which was headquartered in Minneapolis as well. Peavey was a grain merchandiser and was considered to be the largest flour miller in the United States. Peavey had recently made some acquisitions in the specialty retailing area, including a small chain of stores in Canada called Peavey Marts, which were similar in concept to Wheeler's. Jerry W. Trebil, who was in charge of Peavey's retailing division, came to Grand Island and made a good first impression. There were additional meetings and soon an agreement in principle was executed to sell the common stock of Wheeler's to Peavey for cash. The transaction closed in early 1976.

Before any public announcement was made, two management teams, including members of the Wheeler family, visited all the stores to explain the deal to the employees. This was followed up with a public announcement.

It has been over 18 years since the business was sold and some things about Wheeler's have clearly changed, while others have remained much the same. The business is bigger, but not significantly. In 1976, at the time of the sale, there were 45 stores and annual sales were over $30 million. At the end of 1993, there were 100 stores (total sales were not disclosed). Peavey was eventually acquired by ConAgra, headquartered in Omaha, Nebraska, in 1982. Peavey's retail division, of which Wheeler's (now called Country General Stores) is the largest portion, clearly doesn't fit in with the rest of ConAgra, which is one of the largest food companies in the United States. But ConAgra has kept the business for over a decade now, and the 1993 ConAgra annual report states:

> Country General had another record year in sales and earnings. Inventory control and store replenishment systems continued to improve with full-year benefit from a new 300,000-square-foot distribution center completed during fiscal 1992. New and somewhat larger stores that were opened in fiscal 1992 performed better than expected in fiscal 1993.

Wheelers Stores, Inc.

Grand Island, Nebraska 68801

Phone 384-7800
Area Code 308

October 14, 1975

P.O. Box E
New West Highway 30

TO ALL WHEELER PERSONNEL

On Tuesday, October 14, a public announcement will be made that our company will be joining the Peavey Company, a 100 year old Minneapolis based food and specialty retailing company. Included in Peavey's retail group are retail farm stores in Canada.

We will operate as a wholly owned subsidiary of the Peavey Company and there will be no change in our management or the way we conduct our business.

Our decision to join the Peavey Company was based upon a number of considerations. For some time our stockholders have been faced with serious estate planning problems which can now be resolved. We believe the affiliation will also strengthen our company and enable us to preserve the business we have built in the event of the untimely death of one of our principal stockholders.

Several other factors encouraged us to favorably consider Peavey's proposal. First, we believe the move will result in many new and challenging career opportunities for our people. Second, the Peavey Company has outstanding fringe benefit programs in many of which our people would participate. These include a non-contributory retirement pension plan, a voluntary profit sharing and investment plan as well as group life insurance, hospitalization benefits and long-term disability benefits. While our own profit sharing plan would undoubtedly not be continued, your profit sharing funds accrued to date would be set aside and paid to you upon retirement.

We are pleased and excited about the prospect of becoming a part of the Peavey Company. It will be good for you, for our company and for the customers we serve. And most important of all, there will be no change in our business or the people who have been responsible for our successful growth.

At this time we're not sure when our affiliation with the Peavey Company will become official. Hopefully, it will be soon but in the meantime it's business as usual. We're entering one of our busiest times of the year, a time when all of us will need to be pushing hard to make 1975 a banner year. Let's make it happen.

Sincerely,
Lloyd J. Wheeler

If you walk into a Wheeler's today, the inside of the store may seem a little nicer, but not by much. The merchandise has changed, as you might expect after almost two decades, but many of the big sellers then remain the big sellers now. The stores are still known for quality merchandise and the best prices in town, and they still cater to their number one customer, the farmer. Wheeler's is still a healthy, growing company and the founders' vision has remained intact.

The Wheeler's Farm Supply store in Grand Island, Nebraska, in the early 1960s, which was located at the corner of Eddy and Oklahoma streets

MEMORIES *of* WHEELER'S STORES

The Wheeler's Stores played a vital role in most of our lives. Many of us can recall the times we spent there throughout our childhood, whether working or just playing around. The stores were an integral part of the family, and we all agree that something changed—whether for better or worse—when the stores were sold. Nevertheless, we owe many turns in our lives' paths to that sale, and we appreciate the hard work of our parents and grandparents in building the stores, modeling dedication to career and family, and gifting us with opportunity. Following is a collection of our thoughts, compiled in 2017.

Working and Playing at the Stores

> **Sue:** The first paying job was cleaning the bathroom sinks. I did a lot of straightening and stocking, and I was excited when I got to operate the cash register in Lexington and later in Kearney. I learned how to write checks very well because many of the farmers often had gnarled fingers and hands, missing thumbs or even arms from farm machinery accidents.
>
> **Mark:** I'm sure I goofed off a lot while working. You couldn't be around Byron without him creating chaos and humor. He was always an influence in those days.
>
> **Mike:** My dad was one of the owners and district sales manager in Iowa. For my first job, I worked for my dad mowing the lot. I was probably 12 or 13. Later on, I worked as an employee doing tire changes and helping customers. A lot of times when someone works for family, they don't work as hard. My father was the opposite of that. He expected that I had better do twice as well as anyone else so they didn't think I was just there because of him.

I remember the grand openings of stores. There was always a big celebration with popcorn and orange drink. They always made a production of it. The customers coming in seemed to like it. Every summer, we had a Wheeler picnic and golf tournament. That was a lot of fun. I got in on the last two or three golf tournaments when I was old enough to play in those.

At the first store my dad was in charge of in North Platte, I would take a flashlight and crawl into the tires for sale. It would be a little tent for me. But when they would sell the tires, they would find little flashlights in them.

Debbie: I grew up spending some time in the stores, but I never worked in one.

Bill: My father managed the Lexington store, which was one of the first stores. Later, he became the Head of Store Operations. So, we moved to Grand Island when I was 13. He oversaw many stores, and I spent time on the road with him visiting them.

Sarah: I worked there at Christmas handing out popcorn. I remember the smell of the store. The toys. My dad would bring toys home after a buying trip for me to try the toys out. I think my dad enjoyed his job from what I remember. It seemed like he did.

Shirley: I worked at the store sometimes, and pretty soon I started talking like the men. My mother said I can't work there any more if I spoke like the men. They spoke a little rough.

Pam: I spent a lot of time at the stores growing up. I spent most Sundays running around the store playing. In high school, I worked in the Lexington store. I was the lowest paid person in all the stores. I would say to my dad, "How can that be?" So I went to be a grocery store checker where I could make more money. I don't think my mom ever took a paycheck. We just knew that was part of life.

Byron: I was two weeks old when my folks came down from Minnesota to open the farm store. I was raised in Grand Island. I had a social security card when I was 10 and started work. That was just a part of life. In the warehouse, I drove truck. My favorite thing about working at Wheeler's was driving across the country in trucks.

Connie: Even from a very young age, I would help face shelves, stock, and make price tags with the machine. I would help do inventory—the kids were very much a part of the business in North Platte. It was part of our family, and I enjoyed being there. Later my brothers had a go-cart that we rode at the store. In summer in high school, I worked in the distributor's office answering phones, filing, copying, and doing inventory. I even worked at Wheeler's in Kearney when I went to college.

I can remember the salt blocks they had for cattle. We all licked them. There were creosote poles in the store and rubber tires—I remember the smell from those. I really enjoyed Peanut Days, when people threw peanut shells on the floor. We made popcorn in the store, and I burnt my arm on the popper. We had helium and made balloons for everyone. I remember making price tags and putting them on with orange tape. And I would write out checks for farmers.

Steve: When my sister Sarah was born, I was at the store with my dad in North Platte. We always spent weekends and after school hours there. As a little kid I would put bikes and trikes together, unload the trash, and sweep the floors.

Byron worked in the warehouse and drove the forklift like Mario Andretti. Typically, I had the lowest paying position doing the worst grunt work like stacking creosote posts in the summer and loading barbed wire. I'll never forget one incident. Summer time in Grand Island meant 95 degrees in August. A flatbed truck loaded with creosote posts pulled into the parking lot. My job, along with a couple other guys, was to cut them and stack them.

We would smell that creosote. The weight of the wood made one of the wheels from the tractor sink into the asphalt. All I can remember is all the office guys coming to look at it fresh from the air conditioned building in their nice shirts. It was one of those "I've got to get myself an air conditioned job" moments.

It was pretty brutal but also pretty fulfilling because I learned a lot about store operations. I will never forget Buzz working in the office when he graduated from college. Buzz was the first one of the kids/grandkids to graduate from college, so a lot fell back on him. He begged me to learn about computers and had that look in his eyes like he didn't want to have to be the one to deal with computers. I wasn't that intrigued with computer science before, but when he had that look in his face, his interest in getting help was interesting to me and spurred me. Each of us tried to figure out how we could participate in the family business.

So in college, I studied computer science. On breaks, I would come back to see Buzz. The store had purchased a computer to run inventory, and Buzz would tell me about the challenges. The business got the first computer around 1972 or 1973. It was a four-phase computer. Buzz talked about the learning curve he—and the company—went through to use the computer to help with inventory. Typically, computers were probably reserved for much more large-scale operations at that time. For a family-owned business in the Midwest, it was probably unusual.

Mary Kay: For the most part, my dad traveled around to all the stores seeing if there was anything he could do to help or if things were getting done the way he thought they should. As a child, I worked in the Lexington store doing little tasks like marking type fitting, making displays, straightening, and whatever else there was to do for a 10- or 12-year-old. As I was older and in junior high and high school, I would get to know the farmers and their wives and kids who came in the store. They were really hardworking, nice people. Later, when I got out of college, I helped open the store in Aurora, Nebraska, and then transferred to the store in Fort Collins, Colorado, as assistant manager and did everything there.

One of the things I remember as a child was the checkbook rack behind the register. Every bank in the area would give us blank checkbooks. The checkbook rack must have had close to 50 different banks on it. So if a farmer forgot his checkbook and knew which branch he banked out of, you would fill in the account number and write out the check. Now most places won't even take personalized checks anymore.

Lori: We were at the store quite frequently. There were always peanuts on the floor. My mom wanted to make sure people got good customer service. She was always checking out the employees because they didn't always know she was Grandpa's daughter.

I worked in the warehouse during summers picking orders to put on the trucks. I enjoyed working and it was a good experience. They expected more of us kids, so I tried to prove myself. There weren't computers so we had to hand tag each piece of equipment.

I remember just feeling a lot of pride knowing that my grandfather and uncles and dad worked very hard to build that business. It grew to almost 30 stores back in the 70's. My grandfather never had real formal education. I don't think he went past sixth grade. But he had a very strong work ethic. I think he instilled that work ethic in all the grandkids. I think we all have that honesty and integrity that came to mean a lot through the years.

Buzz: I remember working in the store at a young age. I'm probably the only member of the family still involved in the farm and ranch business. My uncles and my dad and grandfather were all responsible for my education and helping me learn the business. There's probably not a day that goes by that I don't reach back and remember something one of them taught me. I'm very grateful for everything they taught me.

My fondest memories are of some of the grand openings we would go to. Those were events that would involve the whole family with everybody working together. When the family gathered for holidays, the conversation always turned to business. I found it remarkable how well the family got along, how well they worked together. All the members were involved in the business. I think my grandfather played an important part in it. There was always kind of an "everybody's equal" thing. When there was a conflict or something that came about, it was talked about and resolved and we moved on. Nobody ever carried a grudge.

One thing we were all taught was that we had to be able to work. I worked in the stores from age 10 on. It was an afterschool job and a summer job—every year I had to do a little more and had a little more responsibility. I enjoyed that. It was somewhat unique that although the Wheeler family was in the farm and ranch business, none of us grew up on a farm and ranch.

Stores and the Family Bond

Sarah: Really, over the years and even now when everybody gets together, they talk of certain people who worked at the store who have died or are in ill health. It comes up when I'm back with my mom. The older cousins who actually worked there have memories of things that occurred or shared experiences. I do remember the Wheeler picnics, and one particular three-legged race with my cousin Becky!

Becky: I was one of the younger cousins, but they always had a Wheeler family picnic that included a pie eating contest and three-legged races. They really knew how to bond the family, too. I always admired how well that whole family got together.

There was so much togetherness in the family working together at Wheeler's. With all the cousins and all these people working for one common good, you knew that you all have to get along and make this happen, make this work. When you have parents and grandparents and all doing that together, it makes that tie. We're all appreciative of what having the store has done for us. It was just a role model between my parents and uncles and aunts and grandparents, working for the common good.

Mary Kay: My dad was a real people person. Every week on Sunday, because the stores weren't open on Sunday, we would have a picnic. My dad had a large grill called a Hasty Bake. He would grill chicken, hamburgers, and hot dogs. The store managers and their families would come for a picnic. There were games for the kids, and it was just a good day. I think the family bond extended to the store managers, who were like extended family.

Mark: The family did so much together growing up. It seems probably at the point the stores sold everyone went off in different directions.

Lori: I think sometimes there were divisions, and they didn't always see eye to eye. But they had to learn to compromise There were times that Dad came home upset from work but he had to just eat it and they had to get along. I'm sure that's why they sold the stores when they did. There were so many things that could have pulled the family apart.

Debbie: They worked hard together, but we didn't see each other much except for big holidays.

Connie: We always had something to talk about. We'd share and hear how things were going. Even after it was sold, my mom and my aunt were always close. We always had a special bond. Whether they were in Grand Island or in Arizona or Minnesota, we were always together at some point. It was very special. We've all spread out. People grow and have families and go different ways. We enjoy hearing about one another.

Byron: There was a lot of luck involved in the Wheelers. But part of the magic was the bonding that made it happen. After the stores sold, the bond that there was—that link—was gone. It left when it was sold.

Buzz: Overall I think the stores helped us stay close. I think the last few years where we've all spread out has been a little harder. One of the things that dawned on me was that my kids didn't realize who these people are. I think having all of us get our thoughts together in this book will be fantastic.

Selling the Stores

Shirley: It wasn't sad. We didn't let anything like that make us sad. It's kind of crude to say, but when they sold Wheeler's, my husband came home and told me what he got—and it was a nice amount of money. We've always had enough and never been poor or wanted for anything.

Buzz: I think there were differing opinions on the decision to sell the stores. There was a real concern from an estate planning thing that if somebody passed away, how were they going to be able to buy their share of the business? You've gotta remember at the time they did sell, it was quite an event. None of the members of the Wheeler family had ever had wealth. When the sale was made, everybody came out with a nice chunk of change. That was a unique way to kinda cap the success of the thing. Looking back on it, I didn't want to see it sold but it turned out excellent for me and allowed me to do some things and go on. I think everybody would go back and say, "Yeah, that was a pretty good decision." The proceeds from the sale allowed a lot of people to go on and do things they may not have been able to do otherwise. Now the stores have gone through several different owners. There's not really anything left of the original group. It's kinda sad.

Lori: I was like 16, and I was very proud of my family. If they wanted to do it, it was a good thing. My dad was only 40 years old at the time. I think they were overjoyed that they all made very good money and could go their individual ways and still be close as a family. I think we all accomplished that. I'm very proud of my grandparents. I think they would be proud of all of us. All of us kids have turned out well. Most of us went to college. Some are more successful than others, but everyone has supported their own family and stayed close with their kids.

Sue: It didn't really personally affect me as I was off in college and beyond. I remember wondering what Dad would do but of course he found something he was interested in. They grew a very successful business and sold it. It was a win, win.

Mark: I was 19, in college in Gunnison, Colorado. In those days I didn't think much one way or another. I was curious if my dad would continue working. From the vibe I got, I was sure it was a good thing. I just wondered what was everybody gonna do next?

Becky: I was 14 when they sold. My dad just continued to be busy after the sale. He was involved in various businesses, including opening a Suzuki motorcycle shop with a friend of his, selling motor homes, and restoring cars.

Pam: I was a freshman in college when the stores were sold. I was so surprised. I thought it was a little sad, but on the other hand I thought it was great. My dad was young. He went on to work for Peavey for a couple years, and then retired when he was 47. He was gone a lot of our childhood traveling, though he was there on the weekends. So it was a nice thing even though I was gone. It was wonderful for my brother because my dad could be at all the football games and track meets. My mom was always around, which was wonderful.

Connie: My first year teaching in Ainsworth, my dad called about the sale—I was shocked. I probably figured it was time, though. My father had plenty of things to do. Unfortunately, he died when he was 47. He'd retired but was dabbling and doing other enjoyable things.

Mike: My feelings were kind of mixed about their decision to sell. For college, I was considering business management. I thought that might be something I could get into with them. When they sold, I had to pick something else.

Mary Kay: Jim worked for Wheeler's stores for a long time. He worked there until they closed the office in Grand Island after they were sold. I was not at all upset about them selling the stores. It didn't really change a lot for us because he continued to work there until they were no longer in Grand Island. It was a good thing. Change is good.

Debbie: I was probably in college when they were sold. Dad was so excited about it, so it seemed like a good idea.

Bill: I was very young and wondered about my father. I knew he worked really hard. I wondered what it would be like with him being sort of retired. He had a little struggle to adapt. But it was time.

Sarah: I was only about 14, so I don't remember it specifically, except that about six months after either the sale and/or retiring, my dad died at 47. I'm certain he played lots of golf during that time!

Ted and Margaret continued to live in Grand Island at 1915 West Anna Street, which they had moved to in the early 1960s. They really lived only half the year in Grand Island: in the summer they drove to Battle Lake and since the early 1970s they'd spent their winters in Sun Lakes, Arizona, which is just outside of Phoenix. While in Grand Island, Ted went to the office every morning. Later in the day he might stop by the Elks Lodge and play some cards or maybe take Margaret to the beauty salon to get her hair done. Margaret never learned to drive and so Ted took her wherever she needed to go. Ted had a white Mercedes convertible which he drove around Grand Island and also owned a late model Lincoln Continental for highway driving. Ted and Margaret had a pet dog named Heidi. Heidi was a little dachshund which Ted and Margaret spoiled shamelessly. An amazing scene was when Heidi received her nightly serving of ice cream. Heidi was an enjoyable dog and gave Ted and Margaret a lot of happiness.

Ted Wheeler with Heidi

Ted also enjoyed hunting and hunted deer along the Platte River for many years. He often went with Lloyd and one proud moment came when grandson Buzz was along and shot his first deer.

Ted Wheeler and Jim Tuma after a successful day of hunting

Margaret M. (Green) Wheeler (1906-1988) and Lloyd H. ("Ted") Wheeler (1906-1983) on their 50th wedding anniversary in 1975

On November 5, 1975, just as Wheeler's was being sold, Ted and Margaret celebrated their 50th wedding anniversary. Maybe it wasn't different than any other couple that had been married for 50 years, but Ted and Margaret seemed to enjoy a special relationship with each other. They married very young and overcame a lot of early hardships together. They also worked together as a team on numerous business ventures. They were not often openly affectionate, but there was a strong bond between them which you discovered if you ever made the mistake of criticizing one in front of the other. Ted and Margaret built a successful business and were now watching their children reap the benefits of that success. Their grandchildren were also growing up: Bruce, the eldest, had married the previous year and many of the rest were in the process of completing college or high school.

Ted's favorite song was "Born to Lose," which seems pretty funny, especially when you read some of the lyrics:

Born To Lose, I've lived my life in vain;
Every dream has only brought me pain;
All my life I've always been so blue;
Born To Lose and now I'm losin' you.

ARIZONA

In the early 1970s, Ted and Margaret began vacationing in Arizona. In the beginning, they flew down and rented an apartment in Phoenix for two or three weeks at a time. While in Arizona, they met many old friends from Minnesota, including Clarence and Harriet Grove. The Groves had just purchased a home in Sun Lakes, which is on the southern edge of Phoenix, and so Ted and Margaret decided to try the area as well. They rented for several winters and then purchased a doublewide trailer home. In the winter of 1982-83, they decided to have a new modular home built in Sun Lakes, which would be ready for them to move in the following winter.

Ted and Margaret's home in Sun Lakes, Arizona

Ted and Margaret enjoyed Arizona: there were many retirees in the area who were always reaching out to make new friends. At the clubhouse Ted once met a man named Bud Rose who had sold ice cream to him when he and Margaret owned the restaurant in Clarissa. Ted and Margaret played cards with their neighbors and friends, and Ted also played golf - he hit 'em left handed. The local clubhouse opened at 6:30 in the morning and to get a tee time you had to show up in person and make a reservation. Ted would wake up at 4:30, make himself some coffee, drive to the golf course, and wait for the clubhouse to open. Once, while driving to the clubhouse, a patrolman pulled Ted over because he apparently had been weaving back and forth.

The patrolman came up to the car window and said, "Where do you think you're going?"

Ted replied, "To get a golf time."

"Who do you think you're kidding, getting a golf time at this time of the morning, and by the way, what are you drinking?" asked the patrolman.

Ted said, "Coffee."

The patrolman ordered him out of the car, looked at the coffee cup, made Ted walk a line, and then let him go.

In the fall of 1983, while they were still in Grand Island, Ted died suddenly of a heart attack. Beverly Swanson wrote about Ted's last day, on October 26th:

Dad died the way he would have wanted—he had spent the whole day with his family. In the morning he saw Lloyd at the farm. In the afternoon he and Mom stopped at Wheeler's and Buzz showed them the new offices. They both talked about that and said how much they enjoyed seeing everything. I had called Mom in the morning and asked them out to dinner 'cause I was having a roast and that was Dad's favorite. I remember them coming through the door (how we take our loved ones for granted—how we would love to see them come to the house).

We had a nice dinner together and it was nice evening so I suggested going for a walk. Dad and Pete were ahead of Mom and I and about half way around I heard Pete tell Dad to just sit down and he would run and get the car. Dad said he didn't feel good but could walk to the house, which he did by sheer determination. We got in the house, Dad sat down and I called 911. I remember Mom taking his teeth out, but I am sure Dad was already gone. Pete tried to do everything that 911 suggested over the phone... soon, the ambulance came and the young men took over. Mom went and sat in the kitchen by the table and I knew she was praying. Jim and Mona came and I could tell by Jim's face that he thought he was gone. They decided to take Dad to the hospital. When we got to the hospital, Lloyd met us and told Mom that Dad didn't make it.

After Ted died, Margaret continued to travel to Battle Lake and Arizona just like before. Her children would help her get back and forth. Jim and Lloyd had homes on East and West Battle Lake, respectively, and all the Wheeler children began spending time in Arizona during the winter. Margaret sold the house on Anna Street in Grand Island and moved into a condominium on St. James Place. She also sold the house in Sun Lakes and moved to a house which was near the clubhouse and church. Her friends and children threw a surprise 80th birthday party for her in 1986 in her new house at Sun Lakes.

In the summer of 1987, Margaret began to have serious health problems. She was hospitalized in the fall but felt that if she could get to Sun Lakes she would feel better. Shirley and Beverly flew down to Phoenix with her but after two weeks her health didn't improve. She returned to Grand Island and then was in and out of the hospital several more times that winter. Once Pete and Beverly suggested that Margaret move in with them. She refused and instead made arrangements for a woman to stay with her. This worked well for a while but then Margaret went back into the hospital. On February 4, she was placed in the intensive care unit and began to slip away. Pete and Beverly came to the hospital first, and when Lloyd and Maybelle arrived at the hospital she opened her eyes and scolded Lloyd for not taking care of his cold. Margaret died in the early morning hours of February 5, 1988. She was 81 years old. Pearl Holmberg, a friend of Margaret's, sent the Wheeler family this poem:

For Those I Love . . .
For Those Who Love Me

When I am gone, release me, let me go . . .
I have so many things to see and do.
You mustn't tie yourself to me with tears,
Be happy that we had these years.
I gave you my love. You can only guess
How much you gave me in happiness.
I thank you for the love you each have shown
But now it's time I traveled on alone!
So grieve awhile for me, if grieve you must,
Then let your grief be comforted by trust.
It's only a while that we must part.
So bless the memories that lie within your heart.
I won't be far away, for life goes on,
So if you need me, call and I will come.
Though you can't see or touch me, I'll be near.
And if you listen with your heart, you'll hear
All of my love around you soft and clear.
And then you must come this way alone . . .
I'll greet you with a smile and say "Welcome Home."

Entered Into Eternal Rest Friday, Feb. 5, 1988

Margaret Wheeler

Margaret M. Wheeler, 81, of 22 St. James Place, a founder of the first Wheeler Farm Supply Store, died Friday, Feb. 5, at St. Francis Medical Center.

Services will be Monday at 1:30 p.m. at Trinity United Methodist Church in the Gollaher Chapel. The Rev. William Doren will officiate. Burial will be in the Westlawn Memorial Park.

Visitation will be from 4-8 p.m. Sunday at Livingston-Sondermann Funeral Home. Memorials are suggested to the Trinity United Methodist Church.

She was born April 5, 1906, in Missouri to John and Dora Cook Green. She grew up and received her education in Missouri. On Nov. 11, 1925, she married Lloyd H. (Ted) Wheeler at Fort Dodge, Iowa. They farmed for several years near Carlos, Minn. They later moved to Clarissa, Minn., where they owned a restaurant and car agency. There they raised their family.

Mrs. Wheeler and her husband moved to Grand Island in 1955, where they founded the first Wheeler Farm Supply Store. For the last 20 years, they spent the winters in Sun Lakes, Ariz., and the summers in Battle Lake, Minn., in their summer cottage.

Mr. Wheeler died Oct. 26, 1983.

She was a member of the Trinity United Methodist Church.

Survivors included two sons, Lloyd J. Wheeler of Phillips, and James H. Wheeler of Sun City, Ariz.; two daughters, Mrs. Stan (Shirley) Eberspacher of Seward, and Mrs. Peter (Beverly Jane) Swanson of Grand Island; three brothers, Elwood Green of Renwick, Iowa, Virgil Green of LaGrange Park, Ill., and Calvin Green of Leavenworth, Kan.; two sisters, Cyd Eckles of Washington, D.C., and Ida Mae Johnson of Humbolt, Iowa; 15 grandchildren and 14 great grandchildren.

She was preceded in death by her parents and several brothers and sisters.

Entered Into Eternal Rest Wednesday, Oct 26, 1983

Lloyd "Ted" Wheeler Sr.

Lloyd H. "Ted" Wheeler Sr., 76, of 1915 W. Anna died unexpectedly Wednesday at a local hospital.

Services will be Saturday at 1:30 p.m. in Gollaher Chapel of Trinity United Methodist Church. The Rev. George Wheat will officiate. Burial will be in Westlawn Cemetery.

Visitation will be Friday from 4-8 p.m. at Livingston-Sondermann Funeral Home. Memorials are suggested to the church.

Mr. Wheeler was born Dec. 18, 1906, at Carlos, Minn., the son of William and Sarah Anderson Wheeler. He married Margaret Green on Nov. 11, 1925, at Ft. Dodge, Iowa. They farmed for several years near Carlos, Minn., then moved to Clarissa, Minn., where he owned a restaurant and car agency. They had four children.

In 1955 he moved to Grand Island where he started the first Wheeler Farm Supply Store. He retired as chairman of the board of directors after the firm was sold to Peavey Co.

He was a member of Trinity United Methodist Church; Elks Lodge No. 604 and the Platt-Deutsche and Liederkranz societies.

Survivors include his widow: two sons, Lloyd Jr. of Phillips and James of Grand Island; two daughters, Mrs. Stan (Shirley) Eberspacher of Seward and Mrs. Peter (Beverly) Swanson of Grand Island; 15 grandchildren and seven great grandchildren; a brother, Howard of Pontiac, Mich. Other survivors include an aunt, Edith Gutzman of Alexandria, Minn.

He was preceded in death by a brother.

Margaret and Ted Wheeler's obituaries

MEMORIES *of the* FAMILY REUNION

In early August 1994, our family gathered for a reunion at Mahoney State Park. Located between Lincoln and Omaha, Nebraska, the park consists of 700 wooded acres along the picturesque Platte River. This was a scenic backdrop for our fellowship and reminiscing. We enjoyed many of the games and races that we remembered from our childhood family gatherings and feasted on a big dinner in the main lodge. A photographer came to take photos of all the families before we retired for the evening in the park's rustic cabins. Following is a collection of our thoughts, compiled in 2017.

What do you remember about the family reunion?

Sue: It was fun getting to connect with everybody again because we're all so far apart. We played games. Lots of smiles and laughter. I hope we can do it again.

Becky: I had just had Jonas. He was a month old, and I went with a brand new baby. Mom had her 60th birthday. It seems unreal because, at that time, I thought 60 was pretty old…and now I'm pushing into it. I loved that reunion and thought that was pretty fun. Lots of kids came, lots of cousins.

Sarah: Eric was there. We had just met in May, and the family reunion was in August, so I was already planning to move up to where he lived in October. That's when most everybody else met him. It was just wonderful to see all the cousins and all their kids, all of us together.

Connie: We did have a good time. That area is very beautiful, and we enjoyed the togetherness.

Shirley: Just catching up with all the children.

Jeni: Becky had recently had Jonas, her youngest, and she brought him. Mom was turning 60 that fall, and we got her Fiestaware dishes and brought them there.

Buzz: I remember explaining to Amy and Eric who the other people were and how they fit into the family. It was fun to see them connect the dots, to see the lights come on. We played tug-of-war and other games, which was kind of fun. Bill Wheeler and my dad kind of organized the whole deal, and it was fun to see it.

Debbie: It was fun to see all the families. A lot of my cousins, I hadn't seen them grown up. They had games that we used to play at Wheeler Store picnics, like gunny sack race and three-legged race.

Mark: I'm sure I got to see the cousins. The problem during that family reunion was that I was thinking of leaving Dean Witter after 10 years and going to another firm. My mind was on something else.

Mary Kay: I planned the '94 reunion. My two aunts Shirley and Bev were in charge of the children's games that we had. That was a lot of fun, and everybody participated. That was an opportunity for everybody to get together for a big family picture.

Lori: We played games like a potato sack race. I had just had Cameron, and I was thinking, "I should not be playing this!" Once your grandparents go, it's harder to stay in touch as you get older. It's hard to make that time to do it. It was so good to talk to everyone. We picked up where we left off. I'm so glad Lloyd did the book so we could give our kids the book and let them read on our family's background.

How has your life changed since the reunion?

Sue: I've had different jobs and have moved several times. I've lost both parents, but it's still a very good life even with the losses we all go through.

Sarah: Primarily my relationship with Eric, starting our life together, all the places we've moved together, and our focus on starting our family, bringing our two kids home from Vietnam, and now raising teenagers, and everything in between!

Bev: I've gotten older. But Shirl and I are still happy and laughing—not too bad for 84 and 81. We play cards, and that makes us laugh.

Becky: Life was just beginning at the family reunion. All our kids were little. Now we're entering a whole different stage.

Debbie: At that time, I had small kids. Now my kiddos are grown up, and my husband changed careers. My folks came to live here, and I loved having them close, having never had that before. Maggie got married.

Buzz: We moved to Oregon and started a new chapter, built a business out here. Our children went to college and are now in the process of starting their own families—and starting another chapter.

Mark: In 1990, we came back to Nebraska. I think life got more serious because our kids started school. I had to make a living and make sure they were going to make college. It's been more relaxed in the last four or five years. Getting the kids through college is a big deal for us.

How has the world changed since the reunion?

Shirley: It's scarier, I think.

Bev: When you hear of all these shootings and all that, it's just scary. You gotta keep praying for God to bring things back. We gotta keep trying to make things good. Be good to each other. Love each other. I don't know what I would do without my family. They're so good to me.

Becky: I think we're just so exposed to so many things. We see everything that's going on all around the world. At the time of the reunion, we were still living in Wyoming. It was a simple, calm life, and now it seems like everybody's so busy. I don't know if it's the world or where we live. There's still a lot of common stuff. Parents are still trying to be the best parents they can be. Life is still centered around family, but there's more technology.

Technology changed teaching so that if a kid asks a question, you can just google it. In some ways, it's a very positive thing. The world has changed a lot as far as diversity. Where my kids grew up, they loved the schools they went to. They were very diverse schools, and I feel my kids are very well-rounded because of that. It was a different experience from where I grew up.

Pam: Unfortunately, the world feels a lot less safe than when I was a kid. It's not as simple and carefree of a childhood. And technology…I can see technology in a negative and positive light. I think it's a negative from the standpoint of people being on their phones all the time or playing games and not talking as much to each other. Messaging instead of talking is sad. But technology from a medical standpoint is amazing to me.

Mark: The world seems less predictable, but that might be because I'm older. It seems less certain. You know, you used to have the idea that to grow up and work hard and save money, you'd be ok. That's not necessarily true these days. I'm kind of pessimistic.

Mary Kay: We're all more aware of the world around us because of the 24-hour newscast. I think we hear of more bad things than good.

TRAVEL MEMORIES *and* TRAVEL DREAMS

Our parents and grandparents instilled in us the love of the getaway. Growing up, travel followed a set pattern of trekking up to Minnesota each summer. Later, much of the family enjoyed seasonal migration to Arizona, and we've all enjoyed spending time together there in the desert as well. But today's generation of our family is far-flung, both in residence and in travel. We Wheeler descendants live and travel all over the world. Some of us prefer exotic adventures, while others prefer simple pleasures that harken back to our childhood, like a quiet shoreline. Whether exploring the world or sticking close to hearth and home, we enjoy our leisure time best in the company of those we love. Following is a collection of our thoughts, compiled in 2017.

Sue: Right now, we're enjoying traveling while we're healthy and can do it. We've traveled a fair amount in the U.S., took a trip to the British Virgin Islands over Christmas, and a trip to Alaska for a whole month. Soon we're traveling to Africa and then have a trip planned to Ireland. We both retired four years ago, and are making the most of it while we can.

Becky: In retirement, I look forward to having the freedom to travel and the freedom of still working if I want to. We really enjoy going to see our son in Colorado. It's a beautiful place. We like to be outdoors the whole time as a family. We like to go to San Diego beach or Rocky Point in Mexico. I really want to go to Ireland. I'd like to take a cruise to Alaska. I really would like to see different parts of the U.S. I have mostly spent time in the Western and Northwestern U.S., and I would like to see the rest.

Pam: I enjoy traveling. We've been to Africa a few times and Europe a few times. Probably our favorite trip was to Uganda. Alyssa and her husband spent a year in Uganda, and we went there for a few weeks. We enjoyed the people and the animals. Seeing how the people live was fascinating. It was pretty third-world. We traveled another time to Africa when my kids were little. When the kids were little, we would always go to Montana—and then we never left.

Mary Kay: We've traveled a fair amount. The most interesting place we've been is Zimbabwe because that truly is whole different world. My sister Sue and her husband lived in Zimbabwe for two years, and Jim and Sarah and I went to visit them for three weeks. Jim and I traveled some in Europe. We've gone to Ireland a number of times. We went to Australia and New Zealand this summer. We like to travel abroad, but I think there's a lot of places in the U.S. we'd like to see too. I would like to see the California coast, Washington, and Texas.

Byron: I enjoy travel. When I'm not working at Fedex, I'm riding the world out on my motorcycle. The most interesting place I've traveled to is the Isle of Mann. I went to a race there. I rode my bike to Montreal, shipped it to London, rode it from London to Liverpool, and then put it on a boat and went to Isle of Mann. I've also been clear up to Dead Horse, Alaska. It is cold. It's real cold on a bike. I've been to Copper Canyon, Mexico. I ride mostly alone, but I went with a group down there.

Mark: Usually our favorite place to travel is California. We like Ft. Lauderdale, Florida, quite a bit. We got to going there because my cousin Steve lived there a long time. We take quite a few family trips to Florida when it's cold here. I've traveled a lot for my business, and usually those locations are at great resort spots. We're hoping to travel out of the country in the next few years. We'd like to go to Italy or go back to Spain.

Debbie: Traveling has been fun. I recently went to Israel, and that was an incredible trip. Israel is probably the most impressive place I've traveled. I went with a tour group, and that made all the difference. It was a really well done tour, and our group gained a lot of Biblical, historical, and archaeological knowledge. My favorite place to travel is to the lake in Minnesota. I would love to go to Egypt, but I don't know if that's ever going to happen. I would love to take my family to Australia or on an African safari.

Lori: I'm really a homebody. I went to Europe with my sister for a couple weeks. I love California. I go to the Carlsbad area to see my granddaughter.

Sarah: When we were stationed in Okinawa, Eric and I climbed Mt. Fuji. We would love to take the kids to Japan and do that climb together! While still there, we took Hailey to Hong Kong when she was about 11 months old, and carried her around in a backpack. In 2012, our family traveled back to Vietnam, and Mom, Connie, and Eric's brother traveled with us! An awesome trip! We will go back again in the next couple of years. I've always wanted to visit Australia, Italy, and Greece. Hailey wants to go to Europe, and Eric wants to visit Norway and Sweden. We'll see!

Bill: Carol loves to travel. She and I have travelled all over the world for business and pleasure. I think the place that we agree on as a favorite place is Italy, especially Venice. We've been there a number of times. We have very fond memories. I think it's the most beautiful place man has ever made. It's really just a tourist trap, but it's been a tourist trap for 500 years, and we love going there.

Buzz: Sheila and I have been talking about all the places we'd like to travel. I think maybe we'll do a little more traveling now that we have the time, ability, and wherewithal to do anything we want to do. Maybe we'll go to Europe again. We've both been to Europe a couple times. I think we want to see the East Coast a little more, Maine and all that. And, of course, we'll make frequent trips to see our new granddaughter.

Where in the World Are the Wheelers?

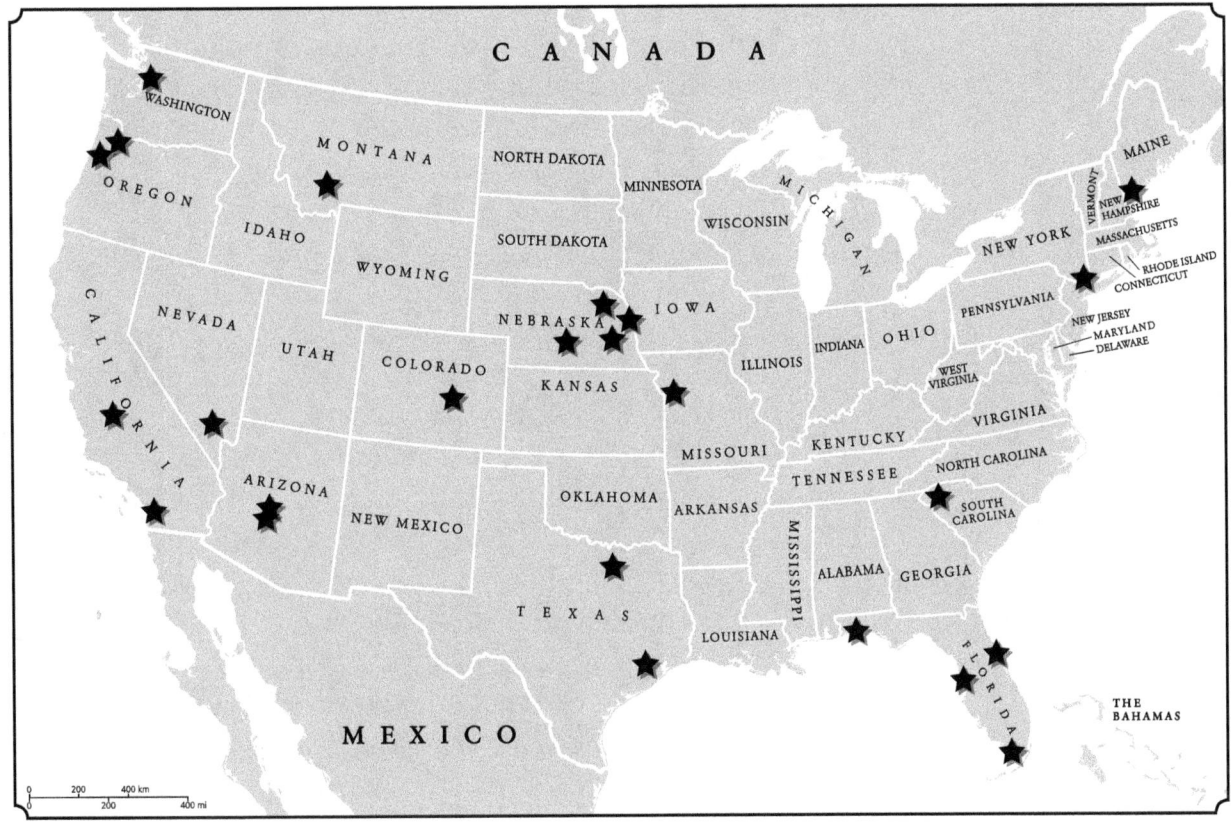

V. DESCENDANTS OF LLOYD H. & MARGARET M. WHEELER

LLOYD J. WHEELER
Family Tree

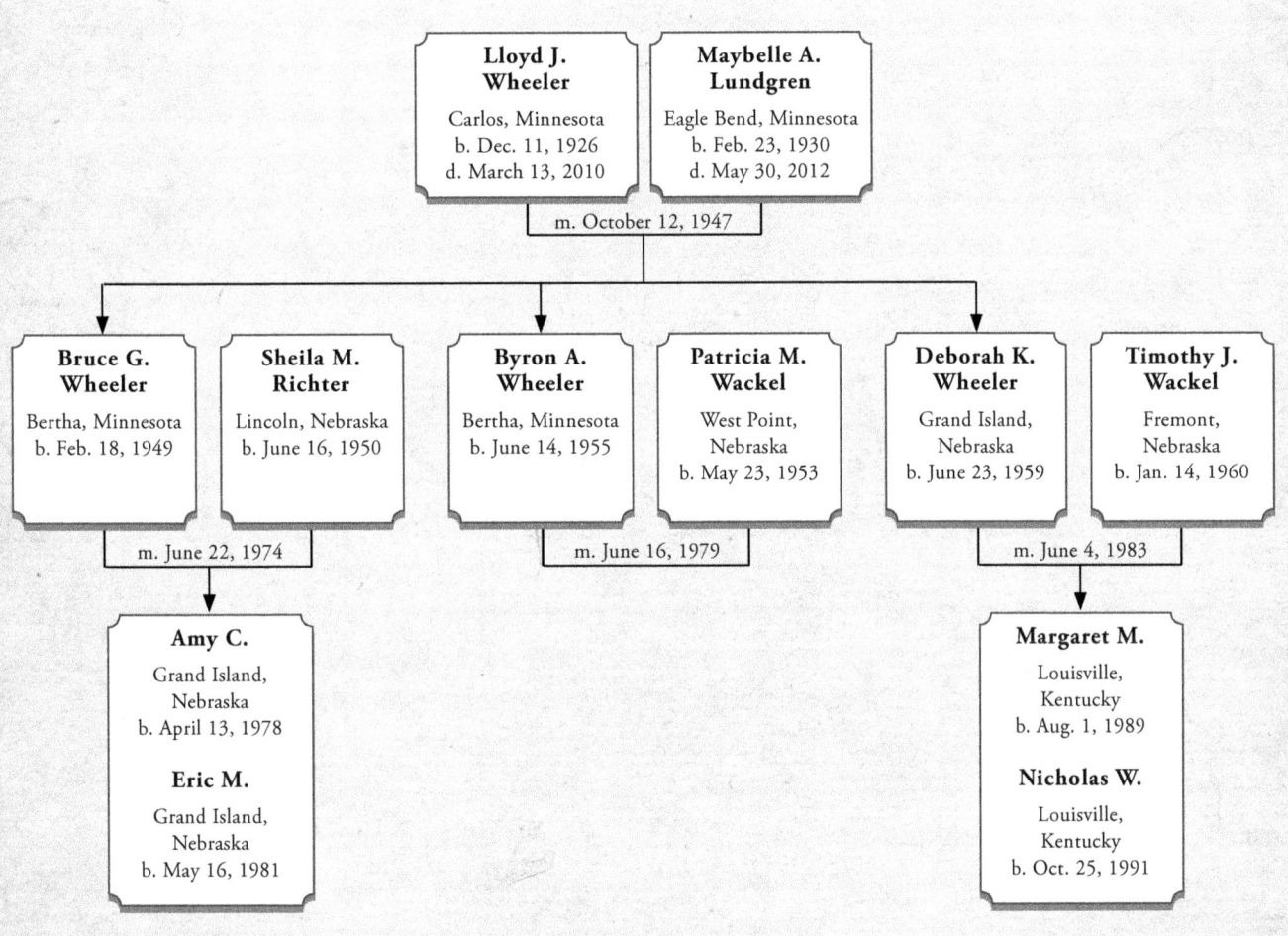

LLOYD WHEELER

Lloyd and Maybelle (Lundgren) Wheeler were married in Clarissa on October 12, 1947.

Lloyd* & Maybelle Wheeler*

1994

Where did you meet your spouse? It was fall 1946. I was in a car with Jim Wheeler, Mona Murphy, Maybelle Lundgren, and Merlin Hayes going to Battle Lake.

Description of courtship/marriage proposal? After our first meeting, I called Maybelle for a date. After our first date, neither of us dated anyone else.

*Deceased

Wedding Attendants? Best Man—Laurel (Wayne) Murphy, Maid of Honor—Geneva Einerwold, Groom Attendant—William Einerwold, Bridesmaid—Shirley Wheeler, Flower Girls—Sheryl Matter and Beverly Hetlund.

Honeymoon? Northern Minnesota and the Black Hills of South Dakota.

Maybelle and Lloyd Wheeler in 1993

Describe the first house you owned. We paid $3,000. It was located in Clarissa, and would have been approximately 540 to 600 square feet. It was made out of concrete block and had a cement floor with a small basement. At the beginning, we had no running water. We did have a pump in the house by the sink.

Describe your first car. We got our first car in 1946. I had the money from what I had saved while in the Navy. It was a 1931 Ford Model A Roadster with side curtains and a rumble seat.

What is the best trip you ever took with your children? We went to Disneyland in California on a train in 1961 or skiing at Winter Park, Colorado, in 1964.

What do you want your grandchildren to remember about you? That we were kind, that they did some fun things with us, and that they enjoyed spending some time with us.

Lloyd and Maybelle hiking in Arizona

> My grandma is my hero. She has shown me how to put others in front of myself. I look up to her because she tries to make the best of everything. She is considerate, brave and never complains. I will always try to be like her.

Maggie Wackel wrote this tribute to her grandmother

What is the best part of being a grandparent? The worst? The best part is being able to spend some time with them. Also, the best is to have them show you what they are accomplishing and what they are proud of. The worst is when you have to correct them and they get angry at you.

Lloyd and Maybelle Wheeler's family in 1987. Sitting, from left to right: Byron, Maybelle, Lloyd, and Debbie; standing: Bruce.

What else do you want your children and grandchildren to know about you? Life has been very good to us. I really don't know how it could have been any better. Most of this is because of the things my mother and dad taught us. I hope some of the things we taught our children will help them half as much.

Lloyd and Maybelle celebrate their 50th anniversary in Colorado, pictured with their grandkids.

I am concerned about the future of our government. I really don't know how to put this in words, but my main concern is increased spending, our debt getting larger, all the graft and corruption and bureaucracy in government. I am also very concerned by the change in people's *values*.

Lloyd and Maybelle celebrate their 63rd anniversary in Dallas with the family.

Below is some advice. Maybe you didn't know it, but at my age, we are allowed to give advice. Nobody has to follow it, but we're allowed to give it anyway. The advice below is in no particular order but I think it's all very important.

1. Pay yourself first. Be sure to have a plan or reserve or savings for later in your life. Believe me, this later in your life will come a lot faster than you ever thought possible.
2. Enjoy what you're doing. If you're not enjoying your work or what you're doing, you should surely be looking for something else.
3. It's important to get involved in politics and our government and environment. It seems like our generation did a lot of complaining, but we never got involved and accomplished much.
4. This last one is not at the bottom of the list because it is least important. As a matter of fact, it may be the most important one. As early as possible in life, learn how to play golf, tennis, and bridge. You'll be amazed at how much this will help you all through life.

Below is a poem I read years ago. I don't know who the author is but I think it has a lot of truth in it.

If I had my life to live over again,
I'd dare to make more mistakes next time.
I'd relax. I would limber up. I would be sillier
than I have been this trip. I would take fewer
things seriously. I would take more chances.
I would take more trips. I would climb more
mountains and swim more rivers. I would eat
more ice cream and less beans. I would perhaps
have more actual troubles, but I'd have fewer
imaginary ones.
You see, I'm one of those people who live
sensibly and sanely hour after hour, day after
day. Oh, I've had my moments and if I had it

> to do over again, I'd have more of them. In
> fact, I'd try to have nothing else. Just moments,
> one after another, instead of living so many
> years ahead of each day. I've been one of those
> persons who never goes anywhere without a
> thermometer, a hot water bottle, a raincoat
> and a parachute. If I had to do it again, I would
> travel lighter than I have.
> If I had my life to live over, I would start
> barefoot earlier in the spring and stay that way
> later in the fall. I would go to more dances.
> I would ride more merry-go-rounds. I would
> pick more daisies.

I am very thankful for the period in which we lived. We have seen Dad using mules to plow the earth and satellites orbiting the earth. We have seen communications where you turned a handle on a wall phone to cellular phones and faxes.

I hope we are still around to see and use some of the wonderful things they are predicting for the future.

Where do you currently live? Mesa, Arizona; Grand Island, Nebraska; and West Battle Lake, Minnesota.

BRUCE "BUZZ" WHEELER

The Wheelers in 1994: Bruce, Amy, Sheila and Eric.

Bruce & Sheila Wheeler

1994

Where did you meet your spouse? In Grand Island in 1968.

Information about your spouse? Sheila Marie Richter: born June 16, 1950, in Lincoln, Nebraska; parents—Hollis and Alma Richter.

Courtship? It's a cute story. I stopped Sheila in the middle of the street in Grand Island and asked her on a date. I made her say 'yes' before I got back in the car. We were engaged several times before we finally got married. It was a long engagement period.

Where were you married? At the Grace Lutheran Church in Grand Island on June 22, 1974.

Wedding Attendants? Jack Rauert, Byron Wheeler, Quint Wilke, Rick Richter, Sue Feaster, Cheryl Troxel, Carol Jo Richter, and Debbie Wheeler.

Honeymoon? We honeymooned in Lake Tahoe. We saw the home where the TV show Bonanza was filmed.

Where do you currently live? Albany, Oregon.

2016

Sheila, Eric, and Buzz

Gracie, Amy, and Andy. Buzz's second granddaughter, Jules Marie Basore, was born February 12, 2018.

Where did you grow up? My early life was in Grand Island, Nebraska.

First house? It was in Grand Island, and we paid the exorbitant amount of almost $60,000 for it. And I thought, "Now we'll be hung with this debt forever." It was a split level, and we had a lot of fun in it. That's where we were living when Amy was born.

First car? I had a '66 Chevelle, and then when I was dating Sheila I had a GTO convertible. We went to the same college and had a fight one night. She had my keys and she took my car.

Career? I continued working for Wheeler's after the sale, went to Canada for the farm store group, and then came back. By that time, the company had changed hands from Peavey to Con Agra. I ended up being president of the farm store group for Con Agra.

Then I had the opportunity to buy my own business, so in 1990 we moved to Albany, Oregon. It was quite a fast move. I made the deal to buy the business at the Denver Airport and went home and told Sheila what I did. We all moved to Oregon within 60 days. Amy was 12 and Eric was nine at the time. So Oregon was our new home, and I began to grow Coastal Farm and Ranch. We started out with three stores. Now we have 15 locations and 800 employees throughout Washington and Oregon.

Sheila has been a real rock in our family. She's moved all over the place with me and made a lot of things possible for us to be successful in business.

Thoughts on relocating? I had never been to Oregon. I could barely spell it. I had no idea what it was like. When I got here and toured the business, I immediately could see what was wrong. That was the thrill, that I could fix this and I could make something go. Oregon was probably way at the end of places we thought we would end up. But this has really become home.

Do you miss Nebraska? We go back to Nebraska. Any of the folks that live in Nebraska will tell you the importance of Nebraska football. I'm glad I'm from Nebraska, but I don't really miss it.

Hobbies? I'm a typical Wheeler. We have to have a place close to the water. We have a home on the Oregon coast as well as in Albany. We spend winters in Scottsdale, Arizona.

We enjoy reading and relaxing at the coast. I still ride a motorcycle once in awhile. My younger brother is a motorcycle nut. If he comes to Arizona, maybe we'll ride together. I enjoy automobiles. I have a GTO—the same model as the one Sheila and I dated in. I keep a few cars around. My biggest hobby is work.

Sheila's hobbies? Sheila was really involved in a group called ABC (All About Children). She served on their board and played an important part in working with them on the ABC house for abused children. She's heavily involved in our church. She does a lot of gifting and donations – she has a whole list of charities she loves to work with. Her mother, who lives in Boise, Idaho, will turn 100 this year. She has a failing memory so Sheila is there taking care of her. I think our granddaughter is going to be Sheila's new best hobby. That will be kinda fun to see. We're to the point now where we can travel more, and we hope to do that.

Children and grandchildren? We just became grandparents. In July, our daughter Amy and her husband Andy just had a little girl named Gracie. Our second granddaughter, Jules Marie Basore, was born on February 12, 2018. They live in New York. Amy is a lawyer, and Andy produces and directs commercials. Our son Eric lives in Scottsdale and is a realtor.

Favorite part of fatherhood? Watching your kids grow and being able to help them. It's fun to watch them succeed. It's hard sometimes to keep your mouth shut. That's where Sheila comes in. She's probably better at that and keeps me on the straight and narrow. I'm extremely proud of both of my kids for doing things that they want to do. There was a little bit of thinking that maybe they should follow their dad in this business, but I didn't want them to do that unless that was what they really wanted to do. They helped on Saturdays and Sundays, and it was pretty evident they wanted to be doing something else.

Sheila's favorite house? The Scottsdale place is really Sheila's place. Of all the places we've had, this is the one she wanted the most. It's where Sheila feels the most comfortable. In Oregon, it rains a lot and gets cold and cloudy. You go days without seeing the sun. When we first moved, she stayed home with Amy and Eric while I went to work. So the weather was tough for her to get used to. She likes the sun and warmth of Arizona.

Favorite thing about being a grandfather? I'm gonna get to spoil her. I've had a lot of people tell me it'll be a new feeling. I kinda blew all that off until we were there and saw her. It's an exciting time for us. Having a grandchild is a big, big deal. To see the look on my wife's face when she held Gracie for the first time was just fantastic. Family is everything.

What do you want your grandchildren to remember about you? Well, I hope that I'm still here for a long time and can be a guiding influence in her life. I hope she remembers enjoying being with me and that I helped her grow and become a great person like her mother is.

Advice for a successful marriage? Learn to listen. Learn to compromise. We want the best for our children. We don't always agree and that's fine, but we end up doing what's best for us and the family.

Favorite place to relax? I like the coast, where we have a house. We go there on weekends. I can get 90 miles outside of Albany and know I'm going to that location and just relax. We don't do a lot. Just watch the ocean, go for a walk on the beach, and go to dinner. It's a relaxing kind of place.

What was the best day of your life? When my kids were born. At that time, we took a class that was called Lamaze, and I was able to be involved in both their births.

What's the best advice you have to offer to the next generation? I mean this for everybody involved: It's important that we look back and reflect on the people who made us who we are today. Reach back and remember those times. I think we all run pretty hard and fast, and we need more time to reflect on how we got to where we are and how people helped us along the way.

Did your parents influence your role as a father? I think my folks were able to spend a lot more time with me and my brother and sister than I was able to spend with my kids. My kids were in their early teens when we came to Oregon, so during that time I spent a lot of time at work. I don't think we ever miscommunicated, but once they became adults in their early 20s, we kinda reconnected. I'm proud of both of them and think the world of what they're doing.

Biggest success? I think my biggest success has been my family. I've certainly had success in business and all that. But my biggest success is a great marriage—we've been married 42 years—and two great kids who are both successful in their own right. That feels really good. I can look back and say we did that right.

Which have been the largest life-altering decisions for you? Certainly when we pulled up roots and moved from Nebraska to Oregon. We bet the ranch. That was probably the biggest decision we made. I kinda said this is what we're gonna do, and luckily everybody came with me.

After we had been here a few years and the business was doing well, my daughter was getting ready to go to college. It was just the two of us sitting on the deck of the boat and she said, "Dad when we moved out here, I kinda thought you'd lost it. We went from having everything to having nothing. You made a lot of things happen."

I don't think the kids were opposed to moving. I think if we would have waited longer, if they had been older, it might have been a problem. In Grand Island, we lived in a 4,000-square-foot home with a double car garage and nice stuff. When we left and moved out here, we moved into a 900-square-foot cottage, and their first inclination was, "What the hell has he done now?" But it all turned out for the best.

BYRON WHEELER

Buzz Wheeler, Byron Wheeler, and Debbie Wackel in 1961

1994

Information about your spouse? Patricia Marie ("Patti") Wackel*: born May 23, 1953, in West Point, Nebraska; parents—Nicholas and Frances Wackel; sister to Tim Wackel.

Where were you married? St. Leo's Catholic Church in Grand Island on June 16, 1979.

Where do you currently live? Grand Island, Nebraska.

*Divorced

2016

Byron Wheeler riding to the north rim of the Grand Canyon

Where do you currently live? Las Vegas, Nevada

College life? I went to Arizona State and studied business and transportation. I took the five-year route.

Career? I worked for a fertilizer company for 10 years. Then I owned convenience and gas stores—four locations for 20 years. That was challenging work, starting from scratch. It was fun, and I enjoyed having something on my own. I was one of the first ones in the area to accept credit cards at the pump. Now I drive a truck for FedEx. It's kind of a role I had when I worked for Wheeler's.

Describe the first house you owned? It was a log house, an old place on Wheeler Street, Grand Island. I stayed there for 10 years.

What was your first car? I had a '72 Corvette. Not too bad for a first car. It was Elkhart green. I stuck with Corvettes for a while, had another one, and got it out of my system. I like the bikes better. I've got some cars, yep, but I love my bikes.

Hobbies? I own three BMW motorcycles. I've been a fan of motorcycles since my brother and I were 12. My dad bought me a Honda 90 Scrambler when I was 14, and I took it out to the country to ride it because I was not old enough to drive. I enjoy the freedom of motorcycles. That's what I like about driving truck- the going away and the coming back. I enjoy the bonds I have with motorcycle enthusiasts. My favorite bike is always the one I'm on. I have a motorcycle out in Vegas. I ride it down to Phoenix, about 300 miles, and check on my brother.

I've run 10 marathons—in Minnesota, Alaska, Hawaii, California, Arizona, Utah, South Dakota, and Nebraska. I had to quit because I injured a leg. Now I Crossfit. I've just been doing that for a year, and I enjoy the community.

Describe a perfect meal? I'm supposed to be on a Paleo diet with Crossfit…but that's a little hard. Once in a while, I'll sneak in a bag of M&Ms. I have gotten into boiled eggs and stay with that and almonds.

If you had another chance to speak to your grandparents, what would you say to them? "How'd you find your drive?" Looking back, in retrospect, they kind of liked making things happen.

What's the best advice you have to offer to the next generation? The best invention is yourself. Send positive vibes. Take chances, and don't wait. Life is too short to be anything but happy. If you don't do what you want, you grow old. Live all you can. It's a mistake not to.

Thoughts on life? I've had: four dogs, four years of college, four gas stations, four million miles truckin', visited four countries on a motorcycle, ran 10 marathons, had 36 years of marriage, and one divorce. And I'm 60 now. I'm going to be just as irresponsible at 60 as I was at 16.

DEBBIE WHEELER

Tim and Debbie (Wheeler) Wackel were married on June 4, 1983.

Tim & Debbie Wackel
1994

Information about your spouse? Timothy Jon Wackel: born January 14, 1960 in Fremont, Nebraska; parents—Nicholas and Frances Wackel.

Where did you meet your spouse? We were both at the University of Nebraska in Lincoln, but we actually met at Byron and Patti's wedding. My husband is Patti's brother.

Memories from your courtship? On our first date we went to Jack's Shack in Lincoln, Nebraska. He picked me up wearing a huge winter sweater in the middle of June. Later I found out he wore the sweater because he thought it was his best-looking outfit.

Where were you married? We were married at St. Mary's Church in Aurora, Nebraska, on June 4, 1983. We had an outdoor reception at Mom and Dad's place on the Platte River.

Wedding Attendants? John Larson—Best Man; Cindy Gaskill—Maid of Honor; Amy Wheeler—flower girl; and Jimmy Mataya—ring bearer.

Honeymoon? We visited a few different islands in Hawaii.

Where do you currently live? Dallas, Texas

The Wackel family in 1992: Nicholas, Debbie, Maggie and Tim

Debbie Wheeler, age 5

Maybelle and Maggie as Grandma teaches her to paint china

Grandma and Papa (Lloyd and Maybelle) with Nicholas and Maggie on the dock at Battle Lake

Maggie and Nicholas on the dock at Battle Lake

Nicholas and Lloyd fish in Minnesota

2016

Nicholas Wackel, Tim Wackel, Maggie Bullock, Jonathan Bullock, and Debbie Wackel at Jonathan and Maggie's wedding in 2014

Where do you currently live? Dallas. I love Dallas—it has a Midwest attitude, and the people are friendly. It feels like home to us now.

College? University of Nebraska

Career? My first teaching job was in West Point, Nebraska. I've since taught both in Indianapolis, Indiana, and Louisville, Kentucky. After teaching for eight years, I took time off to be with my children when they were born. Now that my kids have grown, I've gone back to teaching at a small school in Dallas.

First car? I had my dream car, which was a blue Volkswagen bug.

First house? Our first house was in Louisville, Kentucky, when we were newly married.

Where have you lived? I grew up in Grand Island, then moved with my husband to Indianapolis, Louisville, and Dallas. My kids were born in Louisville, and we've lived in Dallas since 1994.

Do you miss Nebraska? I miss the simplicity of Nebraska and how down-to-earth people are, but I don't miss the cold winters!

What are some of your favorite memories from your childhood? Swimming in our backyard pool at the house on Charles Street and visiting Minnesota every summer. We spent time with Grandma and Grandpa Wheeler at Battle Lake and visited the Einerwold farm in Eagle Bend.

How has the world changed since your childhood? The world is moving at a faster pace and we are inundated with information from new technology all the time. Sadly, my kids couldn't go out to play like we did. We played all day and didn't go home until the church bells rang at six.

Tim's career highlights? Tim graduated from the University of Nebraska with a degree in electrical engineering. His first job was at Hewlett-Packard. After 10 years at Hewlett-Packard, Tim went to work for himself as a speaker and sales trainer.

Tim's hobbies? Tim is an avid golfer and enjoys trips with friends to golf new courses.

Debbie's hobbies? I like to golf, read, quilt, and play bridge.

Children? I have two awesome kids. My oldest is Margaret Maybelle. She studied education at Texas Christian University and now teaches elementary school. She married her husband, Jonathan Bullock, on June 28, 2014. They live in Fort Worth, Texas, and just bought their first house together. Jonathan works for Cardinal Health as a sales representative. My son, Nicholas, graduated from the University of Alabama in 2015, with a degree in Aerospace Engineering. He works in Houston for National Oilwell Varco.

What was the best day of your life? The day my kids were born.

What does it mean to be a Wheeler descendant? To me, being a Wheeler descendant means coming from a family of hard working entrepreneurs who believed in treating people fairly.

What traits from your parents do you have? Talking to people, making people feel welcome, and being truly interested in other people's lives. My parents were generous and humble and I'd like to think that they passed those traits down to me. My mom was people-smart and had a common sense wisdom that's invaluable. My dad was a lifelong learner. He was always interested in meeting new people and hearing about new ideas.

What is the best part about being a parent? The amazing feeling of unconditional love you have for this little person. I love watching them learn.

What is the most challenging part of parenting? The challenging part of parenting was supporting your kids while still allowing them to learn on their own.

What parenting advice would you offer to new parents? Spend a lot of quality time with your kids and read to them, read to them, read to them!

What's the key to a successful marriage? Choose wisely and treat kindly.

Describe a perfect meal. Fried sunfish from Battle Lake with creamed potatoes, green beans, and Mom's homemade rhubarb jam.

JAMES H. WHEELER
Family Tree

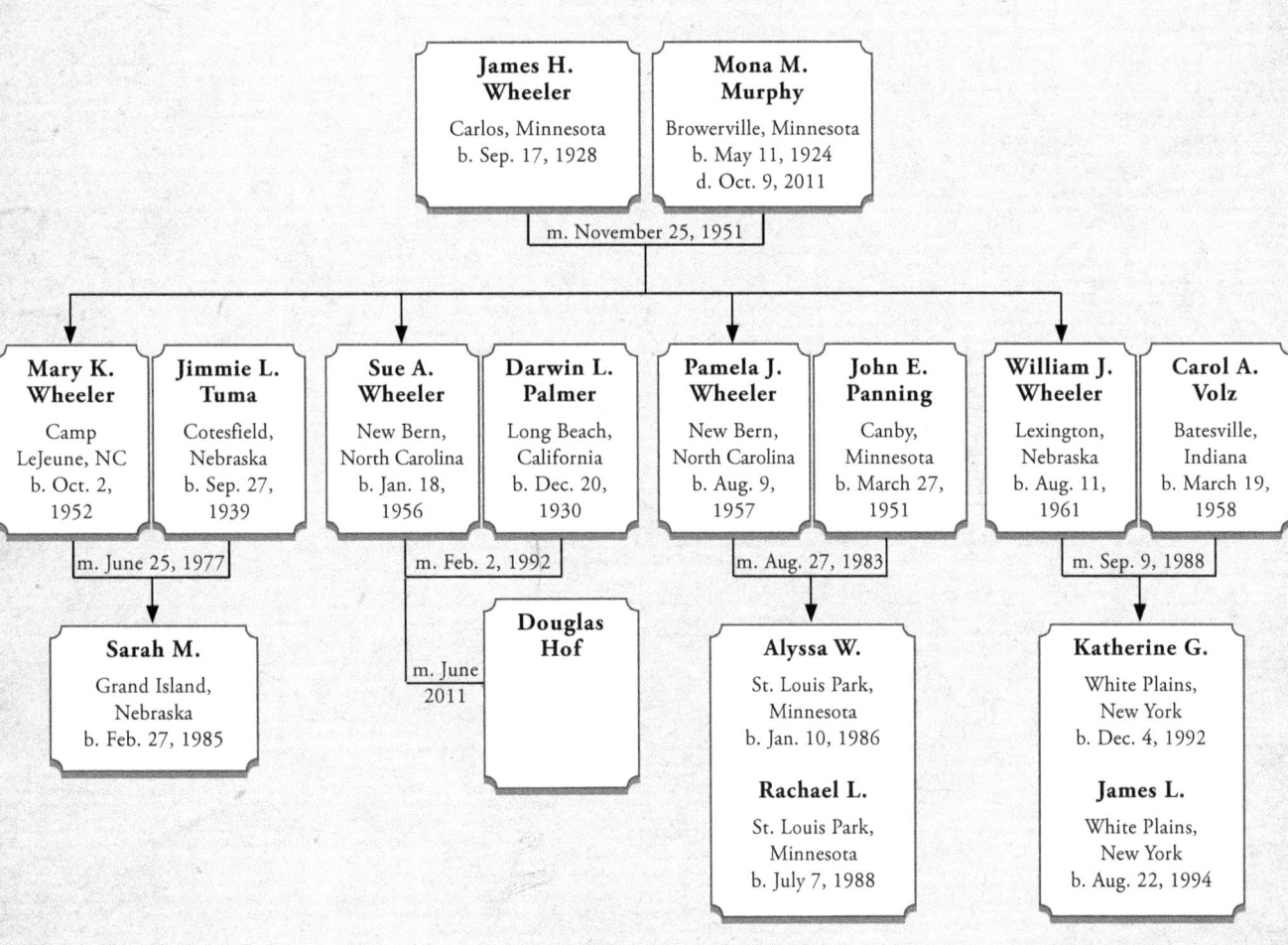

JIM WHEELER

Mona (Murphy) Wheeler and Jim Wheeler were married in Clarissa on November 25, 1951.

Jim & Mona Wheeler*

1994

Description of courtship/marriage proposal. Long.

Wedding Attendants? Wayne Murphy and Beverly Wheeler

*Deceased

Jim and Mona Wheeler in 1992

Honeymoon? From Clarissa down through Memphis, New Orleans, Brownsville, Matamoros, Monterey, back up through Kansas City. Took about a month.

Describe the first house you owned. We bought a used mobile home and had it moved to Queen's Creek in New Bern, North Carolina (which was later destroyed by a hurricane). It was only 8 feet wide and 23 feet long. We paid $2,300. We paid $9,200 for our first house in New Bern, which had about 900 square feet.

Describe your first car. A 1934 black Plymouth coupe I bought used from Merk Medalen (the high school principal) in 1945. I paid $325.

What is the best trip you ever took with your children? Skiing in Colorado or staying at Murphy's cabin on West Battle Lake.

What do you want your grandchildren to remember about you? I would hope they'd remember that we were happy—and we were always glad to see them.

The Wheeler family at Sue's wedding in 1992. From left to right: John Panning, Rachael Panning, Pam (Wheeler) Panning, Bill Wheeler, Carol (Volz) Wheeler, Alyssa Panning, Sue (Wheeler) Palmer, Darwin Palmer, Mona (Murphy) Wheeler, Jim Wheeler, Sarah Tuma, Mary Kay (Wheeler) Tuma, and Jim Tuma.

What is the best part of being a grandparent? The worst? The best part is watching how well our children are teaching and training their children. If there are any negatives, we haven't seen them yet.

What was the best day of your life? The day I got out of the Marine Corps.

What else do you want your children and grandchildren to know about you? I wish I would have given more thought to education when I was young—also wish I could have spent more time with my family during my working years. But otherwise, I don't think I would have changed anything in my life.

Where do you currently live? Sun City, Arizona, and East Battle Lake, Minnesota.

MARY KAY WHEELER

Mary Kay (Wheeler) Tuma and Jim Tuma were married on June 25, 1977.

Jim & Mary Kay Tuma

1994

Where did you meet your spouse? In the Wheeler's purchasing department in 1976.

Courtship? He had worked at Wheeler's in the offices. I had known him for a long time. Actually, I think we were at a Wheeler store annual banquet in Kearney, Nebraska, and he proposed.

Information about your spouse? Jimmie Lee Tuma: born September 27, 1939, in Cotesfield, Nebraska; parents—Clarence ("Bud") Paul Tuma and Francis Lulu Klein Tuma.

Where were you married? On Jim and Mona Wheeler's patio in Grand Island on June 25, 1977.

Wedding Attendants? Bruce Wheeler, Mike Tuma, Sue Wheeler, and Pam Wheeler.

Honeymoon? We went to Johnson Lake near Lexington for the weekend.

The Tuma family in 1993: Jim, Mary Kay, and Sarah

2016

Where did you grow up? I was born in North Carolina but grew up in Lexington, Nebraska.

Where do you currently live? Now I live 90 miles east of Lexington, in Grand Island, Nebraska. I've lived there 40 years. My husband is from the area, too. We like Grand Island—we like the size of the town and the close proximity to Lincoln and Omaha.

First house? We've only had two houses. We had a Spanish-style ranch house in Grand Island. It was brand new. We lived there for nine years. That's the longest I'd ever lived in one place. Now I've lived in this place for 30 years this fall.

First car? A 1976 Monte Carlo. It was blue with a blue vinyl roof.

Children? We have a daughter, Sarah. She lives in Dublin, Ireland, and she will get married there next summer. She loves to travel. She works for MetLife and has lived there for five years after transferring there from the New York office. Jim was married before and has a son and daughter. His son Mike lives in Lincoln, and his daughter Barb and granddaughter Jordan live in Denver. Jordan is a senior this year.

College? I went to Nebraska Wesleyan in Lincoln, Nebraska, and studied biology.

Career? I worked as a bank teller and managed a drive-in facility at Overland National Bank. When our daughter got to be upper elementary age, our bank required me to travel too often, so I left that job. Then I had probably the most fun of my career when I worked at the library of a local elementary school. I love to read; my whole family loves to read. It was enjoyable to be with kids and help them learn to read. I enjoyed working with kids because they're willing to try anything. They don't carry a lot of baggage with them, and they're usually optimistic people. I loved watching just the little things they accomplish and are so proud of. That was the most enjoyable job I ever had. It was not too stressful, and I had time off when Sarah was out of school. I worked there eight years, and then I had an opportunity to work for an investment firm here in town, and did that until I retired.

What elements from Wheeler's carried over into your career? Always being friendly, smiling, calling people by name, and knowing something personal about the people you work with and for. How to develop rapport with customers. It helped me be what I am today.

Jim's hobbies? We're both retired. He loves to play golf. He's great on the grill, always smoking turkey or ribs or salmon. He's a real good guy. We've been married 39 years.

What was the best day of your life? Probably the day our daughter was born.

What is the best part about being a parent? Seeing your child's personality develop. Although I only have one child, it's always surprising to see in my nieces and nephew how two people growing up in the same circumstances, how different they turn out and how different their personalities are.

Jim and Mary Kay in Ireland

Hobbies? I like to read, and I watch TV more than I should. I walk, do some volunteer work, and play bridge. I volunteer at Goodwill, Teammates, and church.

What is your biggest success? My daughter Sarah.

Jim and Mary Kay in Sydney

Sarah Tuma and Richard Carter in Ireland

SUE WHEELER

Darwin Palmer and Sue Wheeler were married on February 2, 1992.

Darwin* & Sue Palmer
1994

College? Omaha Nebraska Methodist School of Nursing

Where did you meet your spouse? At the Vet's hospital in Albuquerque in 1990.

Information about your spouse? Darwin Lynn Palmer: born December 20, 1930, in Long Beach, California; parents —Dewey and Rachel L. Palmer.

*Deceased

Where were you married? At our home in Albuquerque, New Mexico.

Wedding Attendants? Sue's three nieces: Sarah Tuma, Alyssa Panning, and Rachael Panning.

Where do you currently live? Albuquerque, New Mexico

Sue Wheeler and Douglas Hof in Ireland

Douglas Hof & Sue Wheeler
2016

Where do you currently live? Seneca, South Carolina, on Lake Keowee

Family? In June 2011, I married Douglas Hof. We met in Los Alamos, New Mexico, on a ski hill. When I met him, Doug was on ski patrol, and he also had a career at Los Alamos National Lab. When we called up my mom and said we got married, she said, "Well, I'll be damned." She probably thought I'd never get married again. She was happy for us both.

Honeymoon? We went to Colorado for a whole week.

Career? I started my nursing career in Galveston, Texas. They were so short of nurses that I started immediately in the CCU and then ICU. I then moved to New Orleans, Louisiana, where I continued to work in the surgical intensive care unit and also did some helicopter/flight nursing where we retrieve patients that need assistance. Next I moved to Albuquerque, New Mexico, and eventually left the ICU and began working in Infection Control/epidemiology, which I continued until I retired after a 30 year career in nursing.

What caused you to move away from Nebraska? I knew I would leave Nebraska one day. I think our parents encouraged us to go to see other parts of this country. Somewhere I heard that Texas needed nurses. I bought my first car accompanied by my dad. I paid cash for the car and a couple of months later, Dad and I drove to Galveston, Texas, in my new car. He helped me find an apartment, get settled, and then I drove him to the airport and he flew away.

What are some of your favorite memories from your childhood? Playing outside with sisters and friends. Packing a lunch and walking all the way to a nearby creek—it was probably less than a half mile away but we felt so adventurous. We did a lot of swimming at the public pool and rode our bikes everywhere. Later, we looked forward to skiing every year in Colorado. Frequently our parents let one of us children ask a friend to join us. So we were never a small group going to hotels or restaurants or skiing.

How has the world changed since your childhood? It's never as simple as when you grew up. Our knowledge is so much more global and therefore we are aware of so many issues everywhere in the world.

Hobbies? We're hikers and hunters. We enjoy pickleball and boating around Lake Keowee where we now live. We have friends on the lake so we think it's lots of fun to go visit them by boat rather than car. We do a lot of jumping in the water and watching the sun set.

Describe a perfect meal? We always feel we eat very well. Grilled salmon with a salad, crusty bread and some vegetables, maybe some wine; that's pretty much perfect. Nice simple food right on our deck—that's pretty good.

PAM WHEELER

The Pannings in 1991: Rachael, Pam, John and Alyssa

John & Pam Panning

1994

College? University of Nebraska. I studied business.

Career? I worked for a year in Texas and then went back to Minneapolis for computer school. I got a degree in computer science and worked as a programmer. Computer sales, training, and programming was my career, but I only did it until my daughter was one. Then I stopped working and stayed home.

Where did you meet your spouse? While working at Electric Machinery in Minneapolis in 1979.

Information about your spouse? John Earl Panning: born March 27, 1951, in Canby, Minnesota; parents—Harold and Louise Panning.

Where were you married? In Wayzata, Minnesota, on August 27, 1983.

Wedding Attendants? Joe Scheitlen, Bill Hejney, Mary Kay Tuma, and Sue Wheeler.

Honeymoon? We went to Boundary Waters in Northern Minnesota on a houseboat.

Children? Alyssa and Rachael Lynn

Alyssa is married to Lincoln Pac, and they live in Seattle. They have a little boy, Ulysses, who is four months old. They are big outdoors people—hikers, climbers, backpackers. Alyssa works with a community health center. Lincoln is in a residency in pathology. Alyssa's hobby is geology.

Rachael is living here in Big Sky right now. She is a brain cancer survivor. We just celebrated a year since she had brain surgery. That really consumed our lives. She's doing amazingly well. She's a real outdoors person too—a mountain biker, road biker, pickleball player. She enjoys hiking and golfing.

Where do you currently live? Ladysmith, Wisconsin.

What caused you to move from Nebraska? As a child, we lived in Lexington. Then my parents moved to Grand Island after I got out of high school, and then they retired to Minnesota and Arizona. So I had no tie to a hometown. Growing up it was interesting—my parents always stressed to go out and be on your own and find your own way. My dad was in the service, so they had branched away from their families.

2016

Lincoln Pac, Alyssa Pac, Rachael Panning, Pam Panning, John Panning

Where do you currently live? Half the year in Bradenton, Florida, and half the year in Big Sky, Montana.

What are some favorite family memories? I had a great life growing up. We went to the lake every summer. We went skiing every winter. It was a nice life. My parents were strict but caring. We were a close family and we still are.

Thoughts on family closeness? We're really close with our kids now. We were kind of separate from the rest of the Wheelers in our own little town. I saw my cousins really only at Christmas. I think the closeness was because it was just us. I feel that way with my family because we've never lived near extended family. It's always been just us. I would have loved to live near my sister and brother and parents, but we've always had just each other.

John's career? John always worked in finance. He was a successful finance guy. He retired at a young age, kind of like my dad. We have had a great retired life. He loves to hunt and fish and golf and hike and ski. We live part of the year in Florida and part in Montana.

What do you want your grandchildren to remember about you? I hope they think I'm a nice person—a fun, good person.

BILL WHEELER

Bill and Carol (Volz) Wheeler were married on September 9, 1988

Bill and Carol Wheeler

1994

Information about your spouse? Carol Ann Volz: born March 19, 1958 in Batesville, Indiana; parents—Louis Volz and Evelyn Wagner Volz.

Where did you meet your spouse? We met at a party in Minneapolis the night Reagan was re-elected in 1984. We had friends in common who threw a party. We were both invited, and that's where we met.

Courtship? We dated four years—quite a bit of that time was long distance while I was in grad school and worked a year in New York—before we got married. I was very nervous about proposing. But Carol was four years older and hinted that the clock was ticking. I proposed on Valentine's Day. I flew to Minneapolis and we went out to dinner. I was 26 at the time.

Where were you married? St. Thomas More's Church in Troy, Michigan, on September 9, 1988.

Wedding attendants? Peter Ragauss, Scott Hickman, Janet (Volz) DeFosset, and Betty (Volz) Blume.

Wedding memories? It was a short engagement. We got married six months after I proposed. Carol grew up on a farm in southern Indiana. In terms of infrastructure and hotels, there was not much there in her hometown. So we got married in her sister's Catholic church and had our reception at a local hotel. It was a small wedding, and most everyone came from out of town. I have some stories about our wedding . . . .

When you get married in the Catholic Church, you're supposed to go through Pre-Cana to make sure you're making the right decision. We didn't do that. We took the priest out to dinner, and he said, "You both seem very mature. You don't need to go to Pre-Cana." The priest, Father Belzak, was sort of a character. During the ceremony, he called out to both our mothers, "What do you wish for this couple?" I had never seen that at a wedding before. My mother was not amused. He also pulled a slinky out from under his vestments as an analogy to a successful marriage—"be flexible."

The other thing I remember about the ceremony is after it was finished, we walked down the aisle arm in arm to stand in a receiving line, greeting people as they left the church. I had felt so much pressure about the ceremony. I guess it was all bottled up, and I just bawled like a baby. I had to take a moment to compose myself.

Finally, there was a story that came out about the priest a couple years ago. My wife called me and said, "Father Belzak has been arrested." I thought, "Oh, no!" But she said, "Oh, it's only for embezzlement. Don't worry."

Honeymoon? We went for two weeks to Australia and really enjoyed ourselves. It was a great honeymoon. Unfortunately, on the way home Carol was sick, and that's a long flight to be sick on.

The Wheelers in 1993: Bill, Carol and Katie

Children? Katherine Grace and James Louis

Where do you currently live? Scarsdale, New York

2016

Katie, Jim, Carol, and Bill celebrate Jim graduating from college

Where do you currently live? Scarsdale, New York

Children? Katherine Grace Wheeler was born on December 4, 1992. She grew up in Scarsdale, New York, north of New York City. She graduated from Scarsdale High and then Dartmouth College in 2015. Katie is an English major and is still unsure about what she wants to do in the long-term. She lives in Boston now and received a fellowship to work for a non-profit there.

James Louis Wheeler was named for his two grandfathers. He was born on August 22, 1994. He graduated from Scarsdale High and then Lehigh University in 2016. Jim is a Finance major and now lives in Manhattan. He works as an analyst at an investment bank. This is essentially the same career path I followed, although I didn't encourage Jim to do that.

So we have a lot going on with our kids, and Carol and I are helping them as we can. We're not sure about being empty-nesters. I suspect that you're never truly empty-nesters; you're always worried about your kids and what's going on in their lives. I would like to take a break from that a little bit. We'd like to travel more and relax a bit. But I have a job where I'm on the road a lot so we'll need to postpone the empty-nester dream for a while.

College? I went to Wabash College in Crawfordsville, Indiana. A friend of my father's from Lexington named Jim Roberts was an alum of Wabash. He visited us in Grand Island and encouraged me to look at Wabash. He said, "I've never recommended Wabash to anyone, but I think it might be right for you." Wabash was, and still is, all-male; it's a very traditional liberal arts school, and it's small—at the time it had only 800 students. My reaction was, "I'm never going to go to an all-male school, but I'll keep an open mind and visit." So I went, and it was a completely unique atmosphere. So I went there, graduated, and now sit on the board of trustees. I've been a trustee for 15 years and get back to campus at least three times a year.

Career? My father held stock in Wheeler's stores, and he and my mother gave all us kids some stock before the business was sold in 1975. We got cash for our shares and I put that money in a brokerage account with a stockbroker in Omaha. His name was Lee Williams and he worked for Piper Jaffray. At the time I was about 14 years old. When I got a driver's license I would drive to Omaha occasionally and visit Lee to talk about my investments. Over time I got to know Lee pretty well, and when I graduated from college he helped me get a job as an analyst at Piper Jaffray. Later I got an MBA at Harvard Business School and then worked in investment banking at Donaldson, Lufkin & Jenrette in New York for 10 years. I then moved over to MetLife as their treasurer in 1997. I was then the CFO of Met for eight years and finally the President of the Americas for four years. I left MetLife in 2015 and joined Athene, a smaller, more entrepreneurial, insurance company, as their president. As I write this, we're in the process of going public.

I like finance and I've always been interested in numbers. I think investment banking, when I joined, was a really attractive and interesting career where you could make good money. But it was also an all-consuming career that didn't leave time for much else. I'm glad I moved to MetLife when I did because the job allowed me to be home more and also gave me a lot of opportunities to move up the ladder. I spent 18 years there, which is a long time. Eventually, it was time to go do something different. I've been at Athene for a little over a year and am enjoying it very much.

Carol's career and hobbies? Carol was born in southern Indiana and grew up on a farm outside a small town called Milan. Milan is famous in Indiana because the movie "Hoosiers" is based on it. Carol's parents had a small farm operation of 100 acres; they grew corn and sold eggs to grocery stores in the area and in Cincinnati. After her parents passed away, the farm became a golf course. The barn is now the pro shop, locker room, and restaurant.

Carol went to Purdue and earned a degree in Industrial Engineering. That was unusual in the 70's—not many women in engineering. Carol claims she never had a problem getting dates because there were only a few women in the engineering college at Purdue. After graduation, she joined General Electric's intern program, working at the big jet engine plant in Cincinnati and later at an industrial pump plant in Milwaukee. She then earned an MBA at Harvard Business School. Carol had an older brother-in-law who had an MBA from Harvard and he inspired her to do the same. Carol graduated from Harvard three years before me and then moved to Minneapolis in 1984 to work for IBM. We married in 1988 and Katie was born in 1992. Carol continued to work full time until we had Jim in 1994. She shifted to part-time but IBM was changing and she found the work frustrating. She eventually stopped completely. Carol works very hard helping our kids (and me) with their various issues and challenges, which all kids have. She likes being around her family.

What are some of your favorite memories from your childhood? I was the youngest with three older sisters. Being the baby boy was both good and bad. I suppose, by Wheeler standards, I was kind of spoiled. I think my parents, by the time they got to me, were either a little worn out or simply more confident about raising kids. I had a lot of leeway and being a boy was probably part of it. Growing up in a little town like Lex in the middle of Nebraska, it was nearly impossible to get into any real trouble, but I had my moments. My strongest memory was the sense of freedom I had. I could get on my bike and go anywhere, anytime. It wasn't really different when I got my driver's license in GI.

I would see my cousins at least twice a year. We would drive to Grand Island at Thanksgiving and Christmas and meet at my grandparents. At Thanksgiving there was always the Nebraska-Oklahoma game on TV and at Christmas a scary Santa would give out presents to all the cousins.

SHIRLEY A. EBERSPACHER
Family Tree

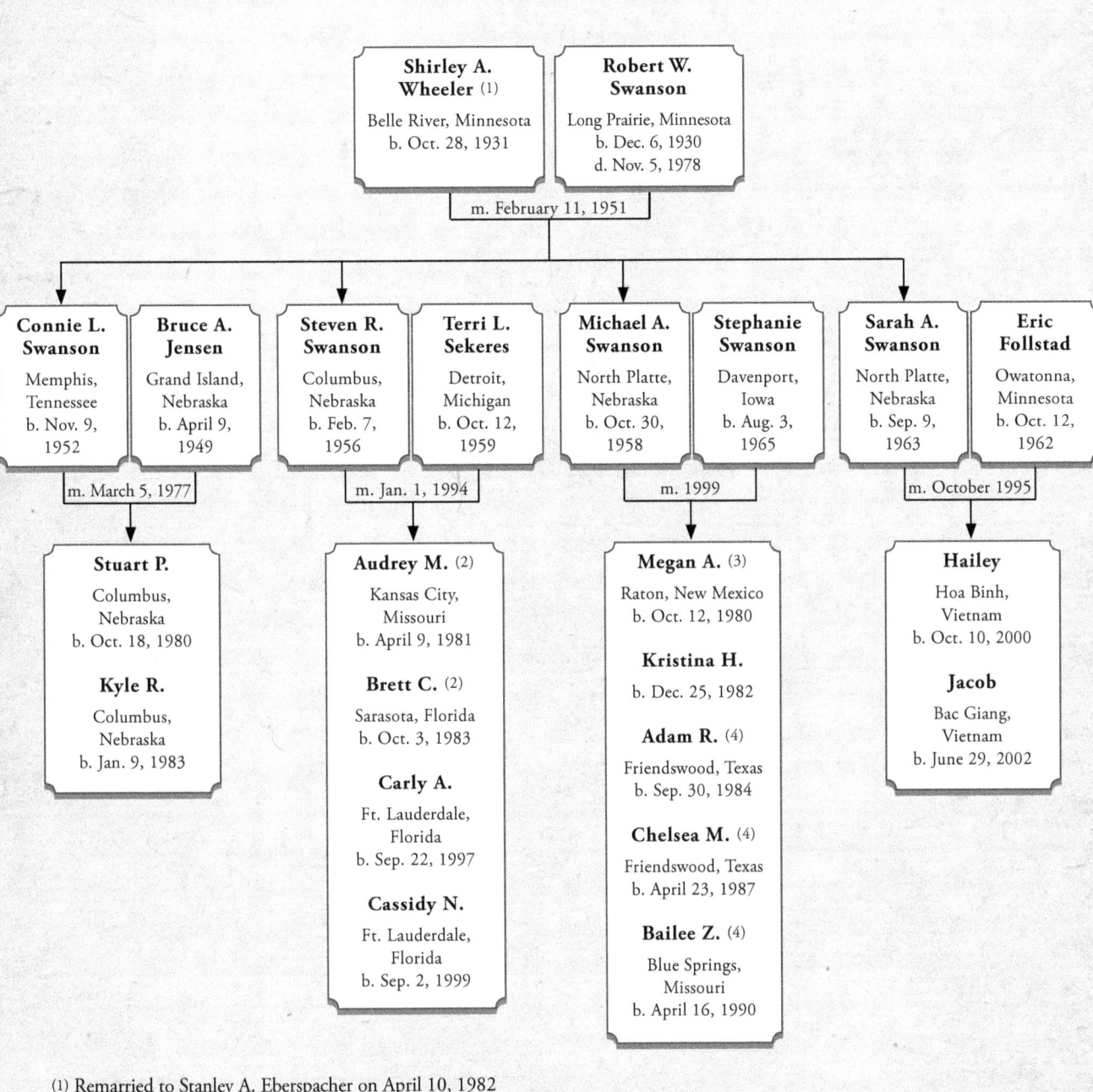

(1) Remarried to Stanley A. Eberspacher on April 10, 1982
    (b. July 13, 1934 in Seward, Nebraska)
(2) Mother is Janet Mounty, Steven's first wife
(3) Mother is Linda Lewis, Michael's first wife
(4) Mother is Robin Lane, Michael's second wife

SHIRLEY WHEELER

Bob and Shirley (Wheeler) Swanson were married in Clarissa on February 11, 1951.

Bob* & Shirley Swanson

1994

Where did you meet your spouse? Bob was a year ahead of me in school in Clarissa.

Description of courtship/marriage proposal? I probably noticed him in '43 or when I was in sixth grade. Once, I moved my arm over broken glass in the garage, and I hurt my arm.

**Deceased*

The Swanson children in 1965

I couldn't deliver my newspaper route. My dad went and got this Bob Swanson to deliver papers. I was really angry and said I didn't want that boy using my bike for deliveries. We went together from then on all through high school. We had a nice courtship. When we decided we wanted to marry, I suggested he ask Dad and he did: Mom said it was probably as embarrassing for Dad as it was for Bob.

Wedding attendants? Max Langendorf (Best Man), Gerald Kintop (Groomsman), Kenneth Kaliher (Ring Bearer), Beverly Wheeler (Maid of Honor), Darlene Swanson (Bridesmaid), and Carol Swanson (Flower girl).

Honeymoon? Minneapolis, Minnesota. We stayed at the Leamington Hotel, saw the Lakers play basketball, and went to a Shakespeare play, "As You Like It," which starred Katharine Hepburn. This was a big deal for us.

Describe the first house you owned? We paid $18,500 for a new home in North Platte, Nebraska. Dad suggested we put air in, but we thought we shouldn't go over $18,000. We were so surprised as Dad didn't usually say what to do.

Describe your first car? Bob had a '29 Model A before we were married, and then a Ford Coupe, probably a '39 with a rumble seat. Real neat!

What is the best trip you ever took with your children? In 1968, we all flew to California to go to Disneyland, and as I remember, it was great!

What did you do to punish your children? I have to say I used a metal spatula or my children will tell you about it. Later we grounded them.

Stan & Shirley Eberspacher

Shirley and Stan Eberspacher were married on April 10, 1982

Information about your spouse? Stanley Arthur Eberspacher: born July 13, 1934, in Seward, Nebraska; parents—Homer Henry Eberspacher and Bernidene Lorraine Madison Eberspacher.

Where did you meet your spouse? In August 1981 in Atlantic, Iowa: We met at a hog roast at Brook and Lana Tanner's farm. We were introduced by Warren and Helen Hutchinson. At the hog roast, I said I didn't want a lot of bread. So he picked up my bread and threw it in the fire!

Where were you married? At the home of Bruce and Connie Jensen on April 10, 1982.

Wedding attendants? Warren and Helen Hutchinson.

What do you want your grandchildren to remember about you? That I love them very much! They are a very important part of my life, and I pray they will ask God to be an important part of their life.

What is the best part of being a grandparent? Almost everything! It is great to see them grow and learn. It is so much fun to see some of their participation in sports and even better to be able to golf with them. So far, there's no "worst part."

Where do you currently live? Seward, Nebraska, and Sun Lakes, Arizona.

2016

Shirley with her children and grandchildren (and great-grands too) at her 80th birthday party in 2011

Connie, Mike, Shirley, Steve, and Sarah enjoy time together.

Childhood memories? I grew up in Clarissa, Minnesota. It was a very small town with a small school. I babysat for quite a few years, and my brothers and I had a paper route.

Memories of parenting? When our children were young, we enjoyed going to softball and baseball games.

Career ambitions? When I graduated from high school, all the kids had big dreams and wanted to do a lot of things. I said all I wanted to do was get married and have babies.

What is the best part about being a grandparent? I have 13 grandchildren and three great-grandchildren. It just gets better all the time.

What do you want your grandchildren to remember about you? Enjoy everything like what we did.

Shirley and Beverly enjoying each other's love and friendship

What's a perfect meal? Fish fries.

Thoughts on remarriage? My first husband—my kids' dad—died in 1978, before he was 50. It was a shock. I was a widow for two and a half years. Mother always said after everything bad that happened that something good will happen from it. Stan was a hog buyer. He would go to the farms and see if they would sell hogs to Hormel. He would buy them.

Thoughts on life. I have to say that life has been good.

Biggest successes? We'll handle whatever comes. I would say the family and the fact that we can all get together and enjoy one another.

CONNIE SWANSON

Bruce and Connie (Swanson) Jensen were married on March 5, 1977.

Bruce & Connie Jensen
1994

Where did you meet your spouse? In the summer of 1976 in Grand Island at Dreisbach's Steakhouse. He was a golf pro and in charge of a nine-hole golf course. That summer between teaching, I was a cocktail waitress. It's a very famous restaurant. Grandpa Wheeler helped me get that job. Mom warned me that I'd be a golf widow most of the time. But I enjoyed Bruce's ability to visit and talk. He's a talker and enjoys people.

Information about your spouse? Bruce Alan Jensen: born April 9, 1949, in Grand Island, Nebraska; parents—Paul and Anna Marie Jensen.

Where were you married? At the Trinity United Methodist Church in Grand Island on March 5, 1977. Grandma and Grandpa Wheeler belonged to the church.

Wedding Attendants? Jack Hoskins, Steve Swanson, Doug Clausen, Sheila Wheeler, Bev Scheppers, and Sarah Swanson.

Honeymoon? We went to Reno and gambled. I was sick and had sinus problems. That night I had a box of Kleenexes, but I learned how to play Blackjack and won quite a bit of money. We went upstairs and ate at a really elegant restaurant.

Children? Stuart Paul and Kyle Robert

Where do you currently live? Columbus, Nebraska

The Jensen family in 1993: Bruce, Connie, Stuart and Kyle

2016

Sarah Follstad, Mike Swanson, Shirley Eberspacher, Steve Swanson and Connie Jensen

Stuart, Cheryl, and Kiera

Four generations: Shirley, Connie, Kyle, and Lucas (newborn)

Kyle, Amanda, Lilli (8), Abby (6), Lucas (4 months)

Bruce and Connie at Stuart's wedding

Where did you grow up? I was born in Memphis, Tennessee, and lived in Columbus, North Platte, and Grand Island when my father worked for Wheeler's.

Where do you currently live? Columbus, Nebraska.

Where have you lived? My husband was a golf professional and traveled, so we lived near Orlando when he golfed. Then we naturally came back to Nebraska.

First house? Bruce and I built a house in Schuyler, Nebraska, before Stuart was born in 1980. Bruce was a golf pro there, and I taught at Columbus. I drove about 15 miles to work. We lived there for five years and then moved to Columbus and rented a house behind the football field at Lakeview High School, where I taught. I could walk to work.

First car? I learned how to drive in my father's blue Mustang. My first car I bought when I was in college. My brother Steve and I pooled our money together and bought this Torino. He was still in high school, and I took the car back to college. He got the short end of that deal. Grandpa Wheeler helped me buy a Nova hatchback when I was a senior in college. It didn't have air conditioning. He didn't think I needed air conditioning.

Children? We have two boys, Stuart and Kyle. Stuart lives in Grand Island and is married to Cheryl. She has a daughter, Kiera, who is 12. They got married last July, and the wedding was at the golf course. He likes to golf and bowl. Stuart works at New Holland on the electrical parts for combines. Stuart and Cheryl just built a house in Grand Island.

Kyle and his wife Amanda live in Columbus. Kyle works for the American Red Cross as a blood drive recruiter. He has a physical therapy background but moved into this field a year ago. They have three children, two little girls and a boy: Lilli, Abby, and Lucas. I spend a lot of time with our grandchildren. They keep Kyle busy in dance and soccer and softball. He is a golfer and likes to golf—he got that from his father.

Career? I was a special education teacher and taught for 33 years. It was flexible and never the same. I could work one-on-one with kids, and I liked seeing every little bit of progress. At first I thought I was going to be a secretary because I enjoyed working in the offices.

I've been retired from my career in special education for eight years. I taught for 30 years at Lakeview High School. I left at a good time because they were moving in more classes. I built the program and was the first special education teacher. I saw changes through the years, and it was a good time for me to leave.

Bruce's Career? We lived in Grand Island the year after we got married. I taught in Aurora, Nebraska. We then stored our furniture and traveled to golf tournaments from Arizona to Canada. We lived in Orlando, Florida, while Bruce played mini tours. We came back to Nebraska so he could work at a nine-hole golf course in Schuyler, Nebraska. He also worked in several golf-related endeavors, such as indoor/outdoor driving ranges and a nine-hole golf course organization.

Hobbies? I am a quilter, and I belong to several guilds. I do a lot of charity quilts for fundraisers. I make sure all of my brothers' and sister's kids have a quilt from me.

I learned to sew from my grandmother and mother. Grandma Wheeler did a lot of hand-sewing. I inherited some of Grandma Wheeler's sewing stuff—I have her Singer treadle sewing machine in a beautiful case. I can remember Grandma doing quilts and my mother did tailoring of clothes—she sewed a lot of my clothes and tailored buttons and collars and lingerie. When my mother was about 70, I got her back into quilting, and she did it all by hand. I'm just finishing one of her quilts called Grandmother's Flower Garden that she didn't finish on the outside. She did another quilt—Cathedral Window—that I just gave my sister Sarah. Those are the most treasured because they're completed all by hand by her.

My granddaughters are sewing on my sewing machine already. My granddaughters are very adept and comfortable using my machine, and they remember every step. They're piecing together a quilt for their new brother and they picked out all the fabric. They're making gifts for their teachers.

I enjoy spending time with children and the young adults and developmentally disabled adults in our friendship ministries. That contact has always been a nice addition to my life.

What was the best day of your life? There's too many of them. Probably I want to say my wedding day. More come along all the time, and I enjoy every one of them.

What is the best part of being a parent? Seeing the growth in your children and when you have them become independent, good citizens. The hardest part is discipline. I had two wonderful boys, and I'm very proud of how they're raising their children. In Stuart's case, how he's handling a stepdaughter makes me very proud. I'm proud that they made good decisions, and I can step back and watch and not interfere. I have other friends who are too much into their children's lives.

What do you enjoy about being a grandmother? Doing fun things. I took the girls for pedicures last week. We bake things, and we read together. They have a love of reading. They can be sisters but enjoy doing things together. I get to do those fun things and spend time with them.

Biggest success? Besides my children? I've been very active with my church. I work with the Red Cross blood drive. I help with advocating for the rights of citizens. I am proud of the students I've worked with and continue to see in the community. I've been a Big Pal for 14 years. I received the United Way Spirit of Volunteerism award in 2011. I was the girls' golf coach at Lakeview High School for 13 years, and I was nominated for their Athletic Hall of Fame.

Perfect meal? We had a pretty good one tonight. I like to have vegetables and fruit and meat. Both of us are diabetic, so we have limitations. I like simple food—nothing elaborate. I can remember Grandma made sweet potatoes with marshmallows, and I didn't like it. I don't like sweet potatoes. Steak, baked potato, and salad would probably be my favorite meal.

Advice to the next generation? Continue your education, love your work.

STEVE SWANSON

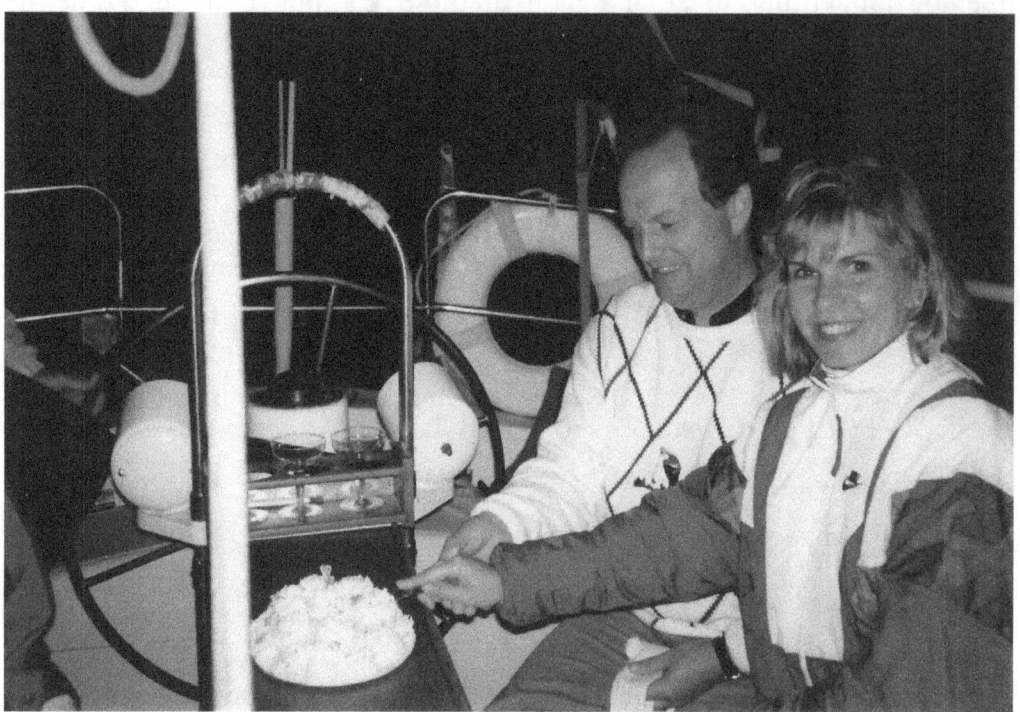

Steve and Terri (Sekeres) Swanson were married on January 1, 1994, five miles off the coast of western Florida.

Steve & Terri Swanson

1994

Where did you meet your spouse? In Miami in August of 1988.

Information about your spouse? Terri Lynn Sekeres: born October 12, 1959, in Detroit, Michigan; parents—John Sekeres and Carol Laurent.

Where were you married? On a boat five miles off the coast of western Florida on January 1, 1994.

Wedding Attendants? Barb and Randy Matooka.

The Swansons

Children? Audrey Marie, Brett Christopher, Carly Anne, and Cassidy Nicole.

Where do you currently live? Pembroke Pines, Florida.

2016

Steve visits with Brett on the aircraft carrier

Cassidy runs cross country

Carly and Dad at a Florida high school state championship

Brett, Cassidy, Carly, Audrey, Bryn, and Brian on Steve's boat

Granddaughter Bryn swipes Steve's glasses

Where do you currently live? We have a house in Westin, Florida, in the school district that is best for the girls. But my primary residence is Marathon, Florida, in the Keys.

Terri's hobbies? Terri is extremely active in athletics, primarily coaching. She coaches runners of all capabilities but especially runners wishing to qualify and do best times in the Boston Marathon. She has qualified for the Boston Marathon for the last 12 years and has run it seven times. Each time she achieves a personal best. She started running probably 30 years ago in local races. It's effortless for her. As she

Audrey, Brian, Bryn and Grant

continued to perform well, other people asked her to coach them. She's got a great training group of people in South Florida who depend on her, and she absolutely loves that.

Terri goes to a lot of these marathons all over the country. She runs anywhere from three to five marathons a year. Once she did the Boston Marathon on a Monday and Bay to Breakers in San Francisco on a Saturday.

Hobbies? I ran six marathons. We would literally go on marathon trips to different cities, but there is absolutely nothing about marathons that I like. I've got my own sports that I love: mountain climbing and Crossfit. The athletic focus that Terri has and her pursuit of health and fitness has greatly influenced all of our kids and our lifestyle.

When Carly was doing swimming, I was "voluntold" to be a swim official and that was kind of fun. I just kind of enjoyed learning and enforcing the rules. I got evaluated and promoted in USA Swimming to the point where I'm a national deck official. I officiated these last two years at six different events where Olympic team qualifiers established their time to go to Rio. Swim officiating is kind of an expensive hobby.

Children? Audrey is married to Brian, and they have two children—Bryn and Grant, who are three and a half and six months old. They live in Orlando. She works for Sun Bank in their marketing department and she helps with marketing to the bank's high end customers. She does VIP hospitality with sporting events and the naming of athletic stadiums and VIP suites in various arenas.

Brett lives in San Diego, where he is 100 percent enjoying the Southern California lifestyle with the beach and surfing and skateboarding. He has his own business detailing exotic automobiles like Ferraris, Lamborghinis, and Bentleys. Interestingly enough, after the last book Brett served six years in the Navy as an air traffic controller. Every parent is worried about their son or daughter who goes off to serve, but I thought maybe air traffic control would be safe. He was in Afghanistan for a year, where he was forward air traffic control on the ground close to Iran. He assisted with many a night mission. After one particular instance he's never fully explained, he won a commendation for air controllers for all of the military for something he did in Afghanistan. He's never said he's had close calls, but he was out there in the dark helping land helicopters in night missions. He always had a fair amount of support personnel around him.

Carly is a freshman in college. She is doing pre-med at the University of West Florida in Pensacola. She did about eight years of swimming through high school. That was totally consuming.

Cassidy is 17 and a junior in high school. She's a total free spirit. She did basketball and cross country. She's kinda out of sports and diving into the educational piece of getting ready for college.

Feelings about approaching the empty nester period? Finally. But you know I've always traveled a ton with my work. I spent six years in China, three years in Paris. What's that next big adventure?

Childhood Memories? I was born in Columbus, Nebraska, spent a little time in Grand Island, and then my first memories are in North Platte, Nebraska. I was born with a club foot and the doctor sent me home in a cast. For nine months of the year, I wore a cast. The other three months, I wore braces on my legs to keep my foot held in a certain position, hoping it would grow into the right form. I had surgery in fifth grade to correct it. Basically, that was the last time I had to wear a cast. We lived in North Platte until my sixth grade year and then we moved to Grand Island for Dad to be part of Wheeler's Farm Supply office. We lived close to the neighborhood with my cousins. Lloyd and Margaret, my grandparents, were there. Jim and Mona moved to Grand Island, too.

Career? You don't think of computer science people as being adventuresome. My first job was at an insurance company in Des Moines, which lasted a year. Then I went to Farmland Co-op in Kansas City. Then I went to a pre-Sprint company in Kansas City. And I kept being recruited to other companies. I lived in Paris for three years in the 90s. I spent six years in China. Probably the hallmark of my computer engagement there was building walmart.com. I helped coordinate and hire 1,200 software engineers that designed walmart.com. I was pulled in on an engagement with American Airlines when they merged with US Air. The air fleets were maintained and overhauled separately. So the project I'm working on combines the two air fleets and how they do maintenance. I travel a lot for work.

Favorite Childhood Memories? I was clubfoot, handicapped, and walked on crutches nine months out of the year. Probably about fifth grade, Uncle Jim was driving through and asked if I wanted to go skiing with his family. I went with them as handicapped as I was—we went to Loveland Basin. Imagine old leather ski boots with steel spring binding on a handicapped kid coming down the hill! I kept going skiing for quite a long time after that. I did two or three runs down the beginner slope holding onto a rope. Then I handed Uncle Jim my poles and said, "Ok, I no longer need these." I was thinking they were for beginners. Coming off of the stigma of being on crutches, being able to ski was important in overcoming my handicapped syndrome.

My parents didn't treat me any different from my other siblings. It was, "Don't steal his crutches too many times." I was sleeping with ugly leather shoes, but I wasn't treated too much differently. I had chores to do, like cutting grass and working at the store. I looked at it as, "Can I get a break?"—and I didn't get any.

Special times with children and grandchildren? At my house in the Keys, every one of my kids fishes with me. My granddaughter fishes with me. All my kids bring their friends to fish. I'll tell you a funny story of little Bryn was she was two and a half. We went to the lighthouse offshore. All the other kids put on snorkels, fins, and masks and jumped in the water. Little Bryn has floaties on her arms, and she got off the captain's chair and said "I'm going swimming!" and walked off the back of the boat. Floating on the surface of the water, there were tons of yellowtail fish swimming beneath her, and she was as natural and relaxed as can be. I joke with my mom that I'm kinda now that Grandpa Ted guy out fishing on the water.

I took my oldest two to spend summers with me in Paris and they got to do wild stuff. My youngest two spent time with me in China. My biggest regret is that they didn't stay and go to school in China. They got to experience it, living in a city with 23 million people. It's incredibly overwhelming but pretty cool at the same time.

We saw the world swim championships in Shanghai. Young Cassidy was 12 years old when we were walking to the swimming stadium. She's the type that can strike up a conversation with anyone, anywhere. She scalped tickets in Shanghai at the age of 12, got us great seats. We got in, settled down, and were watching the warmups and Michael Phelp's mom comes and sits right in front of us. She's a nonstop talker and loves kids. You would easily confuse her with the mom next door. So much fun.

MIKE SWANSON

Mike and Stephanie relax at home

Mike & Stephanie Swanson

2016

Where do you currently live? Kimballton, Iowa

Where did you grow up? I was born in North Platte, lived in Grand Island, Nebraska, for three or four years and then moved to Atlantic, Iowa, when I was in seventh grade.

Where else have you lived? The year after I graduated high school, I moved to Colorado and attended a year of college, then transferred to a college in North Carolina. While I was out

Mike and Stephanie at a wedding in Florida

there, I had a business opportunity to get into a sporting goods store in Raton, 17 miles south of Trinidad, Colorado. In the early 80s, it closed down. I moved down to Texas and worked for Pepsi in Conroe.

College? I was interested in gunsmithing, building and working on guns. Not a lot of schools do that. I didn't work in that field, but it's funny that the training I got there working with lathes and metal working—I use some of that knowledge in my job now. I haven't built a lot of guns recreationally. It's fairly expensive. My priorities overrode doing a lot with that. I have a couple guns I built from scratch. One I did at Trinidad State has a plaque on it, "In Honor of Robert W. Swanson." I was going to school there when he passed away. That one I will hold onto.

Career path? For my first job, I worked for my dad mowing the lot at 12 or 13. Later on, I worked as employee for Wheeler's doing tire changes and helping customers. I did enjoy that.

My favorite job I worked at was at a ranch in New Mexico. I did the bookings for high elevation trout lakes and made sure the cabins were supplied.

Now I'm working as a machinist in Harlan, Iowa. I work inside a metal building with no air conditioning, so it gets warm in there. I've been doing it for 11 ½ years, and you get used to it.

Hobbies? I play quite a bit of golf. We have plans later to go to Minnesota and do a little fishing. We were supposed to do that for our 10-year anniversary getaway, and we've been married 17. Looks like we'll actually get it done this year.

Children? Megan Angel, Kristina Houk, Adam Robert, Chelsea Marie, Bailee Zoe.

My daughter Megan lives in Glenn Heights, Texas, and she's going to college for corporate accounting. Her husband is a sergeant with the Red Oak Police Department They have a 16 year-old-son, who is my oldest grandchild.

Megan Swanson in school cheerleading

My daughter Kristina is married and living north of Pensacola in Milton, Florida. She has three kids—two boys who are 10 and eight, and a daughter who is three or four. She is a preschool and kindergarten teacher. Her husband is an architect.

My son Adam lives outside Kitteree, Maine, and has no children. He does data collection—collecting information and data and compiling it. His wife travels a lot as a food inspector— she goes into manufacturing plants and inspects equipment. They met when they were both food inspectors for the Army. Adam spent one month in Germany and then was sent to Kuwait right after everything had happened.

Mike and Stephanie with granddaughters Addison and Charlotte Brookshire, Chelsea's children.

He thought food inspection would be safe. But he cross-trained as a field medic. He stayed in the military for six years.

My two youngest are in Boy Springs, Missouri, outside of Kansas City. Chelsea is married to Bryan, and they have two girls. The youngest is a little over a year and the oldest is six. Chelsea is going back to school in computer science.

Bailee is still finding her way. She's 26 and married with no kids. She's working a couple jobs.

Stephanie's career? Stephanie works as office manager for a vet clinic in Manning, Iowa.

Stephanie's hobbies? Stephanie does a lot of reading. She doesn't like the heat. Her oldest daughter had a baby, so she spends a lot of time helping with Willow, her granddaughter.

What was the best day of your life? The day Stephanie and I married. It was January in the middle of an Atlantic snowstorm. We went to Des Moines, Iowa, for our honeymoon, and it was a blizzard by then. When we got there, we found that I had failed to pack the suitcases. It was kind of funny. We both remember that. The birth of my kids is right up there with that day.

What is the best part about being a parent? Seeing that the kids are happy, watching them be able to do things on their own and succeed. For the most part, they're all doing very well. They've all gone through some bumpy roads.

What's the best advice you have to offer to the next generation? Whatever you do or choose to do, always try to do the best you can. You don't have to be the greatest at it as long as you're doing the best you can do.

Tell us about your biggest successes? The last 18 years with Stephanie. Most of my kids seem to be doing well. Being there to see my first grandchild and subsequent grandchildren was something my father didn't get. He wasn't alive for any grandchildren. That would be one of the biggest things for me.

Keys to a successful marriage? We don't go to bed angry. Communicating and being able to talk openly if you're upset about something. Not trying to control the other person. There's times my family has had something going on and Stephanie doesn't feel like going and that's fine. Never force someone to do something they don't want to do. We're friends first. That's the biggest thing that's worked for us.

SARAH SWANSON

1994

Sarah Swanson with Kelsey, her Australian shepherd

Where do you currently live?
Phoenix, Arizona.

*Sarah Swanson,
age 8*

The Follstad Family

Eric and Sarah Follstad

2016

Where did you grow up? I was born in North Platte and then moved to Grand Island and Atlantic, Iowa.

Where do you currently live? Valrico, Florida

Childhood memories? My mom (Shirley), Bev, Jim, and Lloyd and all my cousins all lived in Grand Island for a short period—three years for our family. But I remember everyone being there and together, especially for Christmas and Easter gatherings!

How has the world changed since your childhood? I think less family getting together. Everybody has scattered all around the states. Even in our immediate family, we don't come together very often.

Where did you meet your spouse? I met Eric when I was living in Phoenix. He was an active duty Marine living outside Chicago. We met in San Diego on Memorial Day weekend in 1994. The fall after we met, I moved to the Chicago area.

Marriage? We married in October 1995. The wedding was in Seward, Nebraska, where Mom and Stan were living. We went to Jamaica for our honeymoon.

Sarah and Eric

The following summer, Eric got orders to Yuma, Arizona. We were there for three years. Then he received orders to Okinawa, Japan, and we spent three years there. After Okinawa, we moved to Tampa.

Children? Hailey and Jacob

It was a difficult time for us to be in Okinawa. We were trying to start a family and having health issues. In Okinawa, we adopted our first daughter from Vietnam. She was born in 2000 and was five months old when we adopted her. The adoption process was complicated because there wasn't an agency located overseas, so we started an adoption support group while we were there, and met many families interested in or having already adopted. Hailey turned 16 in October and loves music, school, and is interested in engineering and the biomedical field.

As we were transitioning to Tampa in May of 2002, we had already started the process for our second adoption, which was completed in November 2002. Jacob was four months old when we adopted him, and he's now 14 years old. He likes paintball and plays whenever he can. He is also involved in cross country, soccer, flag football, and golf through his middle school.

Eric's career? Eric retired in 2005 and did some contracting work. Now he's a government employee working for the U.S. Air Force at MacDill Air Force Base as a science and technology analyst.

Eric's hobbies? He loves working on his Viper (and driving it!).

Career? I homeschooled the kids until middle school. That was challenging but I'm glad we did it as long as we did. My degree is in marketing, and I ran the marketing department for a welfare to work agency in Arizona. Now that the kids are in school, I may consider getting involved in personal training and/or nutrition.

Hobbies? I enjoy working out. I'm getting back into running, training for a marathon. I hadn't run a marathon in 10 years. My first marathon I ran a week before we got Jacob. It was the Marine Corps Marathon, and Eric and I ran it together (well, we started together!). I did one or two marathons every year for five years and then started to have leg issues. I lift weights and participate in CrossFit as well. I also like quilting and reading and dog agility. I have a couple Australian Shepherds that compete in competitions to include a national event every year.

Favorite part about being a mom? Seeing the changes throughout the years, and our relationships develop closer over time. The neatest part is when there's improvement and growth.

Sarah, Tango, and Keno

Most challenging aspect of motherhood? Mostly helping them work through adolescence and also trying to help them through the adoption issues. That's more heart-wrenching.

Children's heritage? Our family traveled back to Vietnam in 2012, where we visited each of the kids' orphanages. They loved seeing their birth country, eating authentic Vietnamese food and learning about Vietnamese history and customs. Many wonderful memories! My mom and sister Connie and Eric's brother Carl also went with us! We plan on returning to Vietnam in 2019!

BEVERLY J. SWANSON
Family Tree

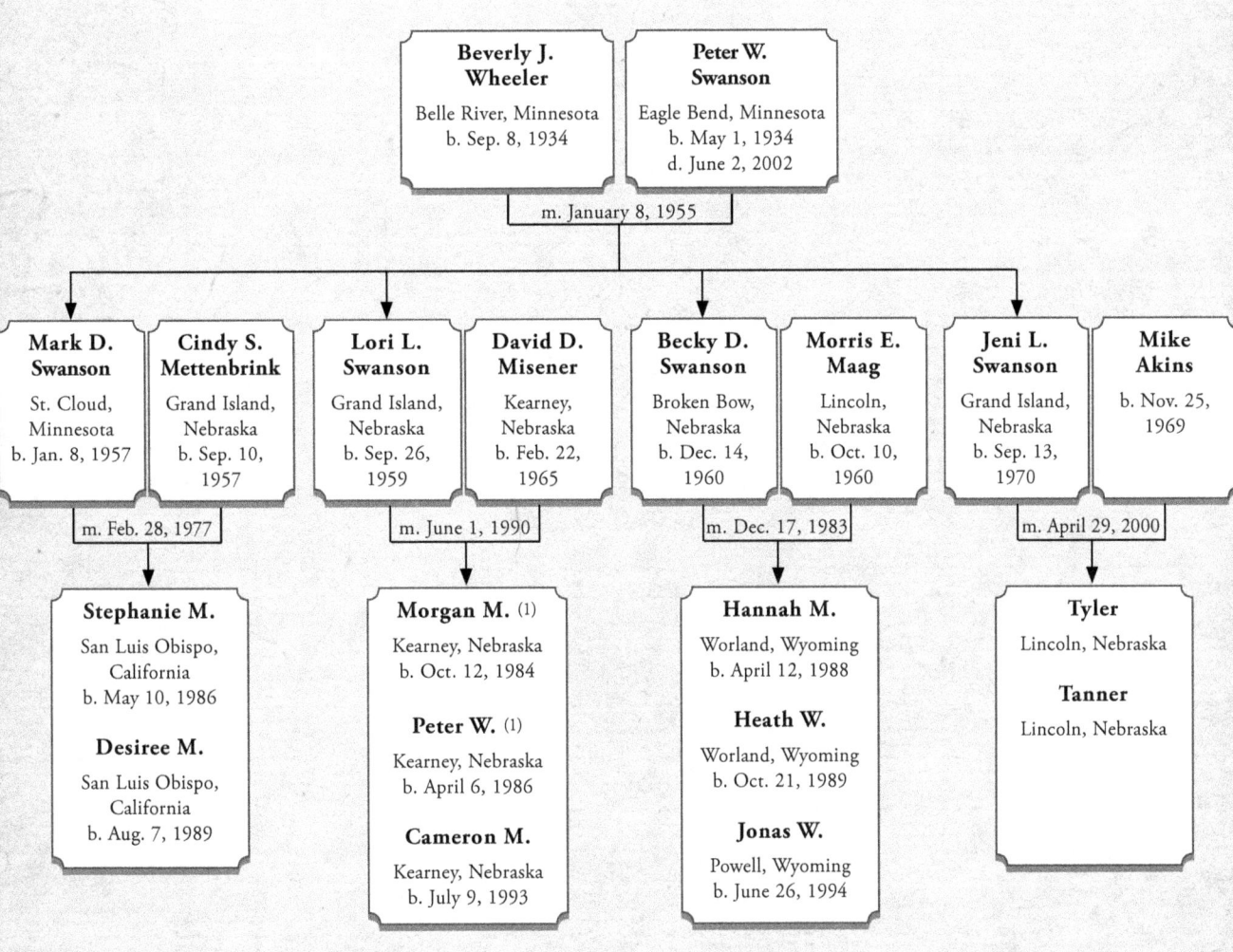

(1) Father is Mark Matuschka, Lori's first husband

BEVERLY SWANSON

Pete and Beverly (Wheeler) Swanson were married in Clarissa on January 8, 1955.

Peter* & Beverly Swanson

1994

Where did you meet your spouse? In 1947, this cute boy would come to town on Saturday night for the free movies at the Clarissa park.

Description of courtship/marriage proposal? We dated on and off through high school: attended activities at school, went to movies, roller skating. Pete went into the service, and we got married on his first leave.

*Deceased

Pete and Bev Swanson in 1992

Wedding Attendants? Wayne Stuckmayor, Lloyd Wheeler, Bruce Wheeler (ring bearer), Shirley Wheeler, Anita Johnson, and Diane Swanson (flower girl).

Honeymoon? The first night we spent at a motel in Parkers Prairie. Pete was home on leave, so we had a good trip back to Texas.

First house? We bought our first house in Broken Bow, Nebraska. It was a big two-story with four bedrooms—3,000 square feet. We paid $20,000. It was a lovely house.

First car? When we got married, Pete had a '52 Studebaker that he paid $700 for, plus the trade in. It was white and a real classy car.

What did you do to punish your children? A good whack on the rear once in a while. I was a mother who raised her voice a lot.

The Swanson family in 1991. From left to right; back row: Morris Maag, Morgan Misener, Hannah Maag, Mark Swanson and Stephanie Swanson; front row: Pete Swanson, Becky (Swanson) Maag, Heath Maag, Cindy (Mettenbrink) Swanson, Desi Swanson, Beverly (Wheeler) Swanson, Jeni Swanson, Lori (Swanson) Misener, Pete Misener and Dave Misener.

What do you want your grandchildren to remember about you? I want them to remember how much they mean to us and how much enjoyment they have given us. Pete says he wants them to remember how good looking he was and that I was a good Grandma!

What is the best part about being a grandparent? The best part is when Morgan wants to spend her ninth birthday with me; when I can watch Pete play baseball and see him kiss his baby sister as he passes her; when I can hear pretty Stephanie read and play cards with her; and little Desi just being Desi—she is just a delight. Seeing Heath wearing his Batman cape and really thinking he could be president someday; and beautiful Hannah sending me a wound up mouse in the mail; and to see baby Cameron smile really lights up my life!

The worst part is seeing them grow up so fast and knowing I am getting old. I would like to live to see them all graduate from college.

What else do you want your children and grandchildren to know about you? I would like them to know that I felt very fortunate to have been born into this family. I had parents who loved me and always wanted the best for me. I had a happy childhood, and I couldn't have married a better man than Pete. I had four healthy children and was able to stay home and raise them and now see them as good adults, raising wonderful children. I have truly been blessed and thank God every day for all these blessings. My one regret was not getting an education. I always wanted to be a nurse but didn't have the confidence to get the education. Pete always tried to encourage me, but I always found an excuse.

I enjoy people and am in awe of nature and how God keeps our world working. I am nearing the "Big 60"—looking back, I can't believe how very fast life has gone. I have had my ups and downs, but for the most part, life has been very good to me. I would say to my future generations to always keep God in your life and to be good and understanding to those close to you.

Where do you currently live? Grand Island, Nebraska, and Sun Lakes, Arizona.

2016

Shirley Eberspacher and Beverly Swanson

Beverly Swanson

What do you like about Grand Island? I can't think of anything I *don't* like about Grand Island, and that's the truth. People are friendly, and there are enough things to do.

Children? I thank God every day for my life and my children. I couldn't ask for better children.

Grandchildren? I have 10 grandchildren and two great grandchildren. My youngest three grandchildren (Jonas Maag, Tyler Akins, and Tanner Akins) were born after the first family history was published. I love them all so much.

Siblings? All our family, the four kids, respected each other. I have a love for my sister. We loved each other. If I have a favorite or feel closer to someone, it was Lloyd for me. There was a closeness between the two of us. Lloyd was the head of the Wheeler's stores. He made good decisions. We respected him so much.

My husband passed away in 2002, and Shirley has been a comfort to me. Shirley and I are so close—I don't know what I'd do without her.

Career? I stayed home and raised my children. Later, I worked as a cashier. I am in awe of women who go to work and come home and care for their family. I have all the admiration for women who can do that.

Favorite mealtime memories? Before church, I would put a roast in the oven, and we would enjoy it when we got home.

Parenting challenges? I think raising a family is a challenge. The grandchildren do respect us, especially if we send a check once in a while.

Biggest success? Knowing God and trying to do the right thing. I haven't always done the right thing, but I ask for forgiveness. I get up every morning and thank God for everything. I have so much to be thankful for.

MARK SWANSON

The Swanson family: Stephanie, Mark, Desiree and Cindy

Mark & Cindy Swanson

1994

Where did you grow up? Broken Bow and Grand Island, Nebraska

Where did you meet your spouse? In 1972, at Northwest High School in Grand Island.

Information about your spouse? Cindy Sue Mettenbrink: born September 10, 1957, in Grand Island, Nebraska; parents—Leo and Jeanne Mettenbrink.

Courtship? We just always enjoyed being around each other and made each other laugh. Our families came from the same socioeconomic backgrounds and religion, so we were compatible. It sounds kinda boring, but we've had a lot of fun together.

Where were you married? At St. Paul's Lutheran Church in Grand Island on February 28, 1977. She was 19, and I was 20.

Wedding Attendants? Ted Jankovitz and Kathy Mettenbrink.

Honeymoon? We went to Vail, Colorado. We *did not* go to Minnesota. That was a good trip.

Children? Stephanie Margo and Desiree Marie.

Where do you currently live? Kearney, Nebraska

Cindy Mettenbrink and Mark Swanson in 1974

2016

Where do you currently live? Kearney, Nebraska

Where else have you lived? We moved to California in 1979, and I went to Cal Polytech. I stayed for 11 years and then moved back to Nebraska in 1990. We came back to Nebraska to get back with family. It turned out to be a great thing.

College? Cal Polytech. I went for engineering and changed my major to economics.

First house? Our first house we moved into was a house that Shirley and Bob Swanson owned and eventually my mom and dad bought and moved our family into. Then Cindy and I bought the house from Mom and Dad. They sold it to us at a discounted value. It was in a nice area with lots of kids.

First car? It was a '57 Chevy that was in really bad condition. My dad let me buy it for about $500 dollars, and I did quite a bit of work on it. I bought that when I was 14. I eventually traded it and bought a Chevy Super Sport. I currently race a Mustang Shelby GT350. I've always liked to drive fast, I guess.

Career? I've been an investment broker since 1985. I started my own business in 2006 and have an office in Kearney and an office in Omaha.

Cindy's career? My wife is the business office manager for a large physician group. She has been in that career since the early 1990s.

Keys to success in marriage? Part of the success in marriage is luck and we've been fortunate because we haven't had to endure any tragedies that can be life changing.

Children? We have two daughters, Stephanie and Desiree. Steph has been married close to four years and is a trader at a money management group in Omaha. She is married to Tyson

Bloombergs, who sells sanitizing healthcare equipment. Desi is a nurse, and she mostly works with infants and young kids. Desi is engaged and scheduled to be married to Mark Hanson on New Year's Eve. He's a structural engineer.

Favorite thing about being a father? Just enjoying watching my daughters getting older. I wasn't a particularly close father in the first seven or eight years. I spent a lot of time working. When they started to reach junior high, I was in a position to come home earlier. Desi played a lot of soccer, and I was usually the coach or assistant coach. Doing family things was always enjoyable and helped keep the family close together.

Favorite thing about being a grandfather? That's been the best thing. My granddaughter's name is Lilly and she's 15 months old. She's probably the best thing that's happened to us. We're probably in Omaha four out of five weekends to see her.

What do you want your grandchildren to remember about you? I would hope that I could relax and be easy going and easy to be around. That's not necessarily my personality.

What's the best advice you have to offer to the next generation? Pay attention to the simple stuff. Those are the things that you remember.

Hobbies? We both enjoy golfing, biking, and travelling. Cindy enjoys exercising, going to the gym. We've been doing more biking together and taking long walks. She likes to read a lot. Her biggest attention now is on our new grandchild.

Describe a perfect meal? We love to eat out. We like variety. There are terrific restaurants in Omaha, and eating out is one of our hobbies. We have a condo in Omaha, and I don't think we've ever cooked on that stove.

Biggest challenges? I haven't had too many challenges. It's back to that fortunate thing. I've had a lot of luck and I guess our biggest challenge was hoping we provided the right home atmosphere to keep the kids out of trouble in high school and then allowing them to be adults in college. Our kids were easy growing up—we've been blessed.

Biggest success? Raising my daughters. Actually, that's probably my wife's biggest success. Second, I would be pretty proud of the business I started 10 years ago, Black Oak Investment Counsel.

What are some of your favorite memories from your childhood? Broken Bow seemed like an innocent and pretty simple place to grow up. We moved to Grand Island in fifth grade, and it seemed like a bigger city. I remember meeting together with the family on Thanksgiving and Christmas and going to the old Grand Theater in the afternoons while the adults played cards. You wanted to be at Byron Wheeler's table because he was pretty funny and would get you into trouble with the adults.

Mark Swanson and his family out to dinner

LORI SWANSON

David & Lori Misener
1994

Where did you meet your spouse? At my neighbor's in the summer of 1987.

Information about your spouse? David Duane Misener*: born February 22, 1965, in Kearney, Nebraska; parents—Marvin Ray and Patricia Pallett Misener.

Where were you married? At the Buffalo County Courthouse in Kearney on June 1, 1990. We had an ice cream cake from Dairy Queen, which we shared with my daycare kids. Dave played in a softball tournament that night. Most enjoyable, stress-free, wedding ever!

Wedding Attendants? Rick Pettit and Ginger Zikmund

Children? Morgan Michelle, Peter Wesley, Cameron Mataya.

Where do you currently live? Chandler, AZ

*Divorced

2016

Where did you grow up? Grand Island, Nebraska

Where do you live now? Chandler, Arizona

Did you have a good relationship with your cousins? Yes, we lived near Uncle Bob and Aunt Shirley. My cousin Mike and I were in the same class at Engleman Elementary. We spent time together and had the same friends. My parents bought their home years later, which we lived in during our high school years. Our other cousins lived in Grand Island and Lexington, and we saw them mainly for the holidays.

First car? My first car was a green '53 Chevy that was previously used as the airport car for Wheeler's. I thought it was the ugliest car! It was the 70s and I wanted to drive a Camaro or Nova, but not that! It was a big car, and my parents wanted me to be safe.

Dave and Lori with grandson, Ben

Education? I graduated from the University of Nebraska at Kearney with a degree in Elementary Education.

Why did you leave Nebraska? My grandparents originally came to Arizona and had a place in Sun Lakes. Mom and Dad built a second home in Sun Lakes in the 90s, and I just loved Arizona. Once Morgan graduated from high school, we moved here in 2003. Becky lives here as well and we're just a few miles from each other.

Hobbies? I spend a lot of time with my four-year-old grandson, Ben. He's my main focus right now, but I love to walk and be outside working in my yard. I love to read and spend time on the computer. I enjoy politics, which has been interesting this year. I like to read biographies and learn about American history.

Career? I owned my own daycare/preschool for 10 years while my kids were young. Once my kids were in school full-time, I worked at the hospital for the Risk Manager; at the University in the Distance Learning Center; and for the State of Nebraska as a child support enforcement worker, which was very rewarding. While living in Arizona, I've worked for Target Financial as a credit card collector and as an online banking associate with Fiserv.

David's career? He's a commercial electrician and just completed the world's largest Harley Davidson in Scottsdale. He's the hardest worker I know. If he's not working, he's not happy.

Divorce? We actually got divorced in 2000 but stayed friendly. In 2003, he came with us to Arizona. We still live together, and it's worked for us.

Children? Dave adopted my two older children and we have one daughter together. Our oldest, Morgan, is 31. She's in Portland, Oregon, and works as a retail manager for a salon. She is very creative, loves reading and music. She's got a big heart, and I wish we lived closer.

My son, Pete, is 30 and also lives in Chandler, Arizona. He worked as a supervisor in financial services while also serving in the National Guard. He's now completing a degree at the University of Arizona in Economics/Business Analytics. He lives with his girlfriend, Aileen, and they've been together for six years. They have two dogs.

Morgan with her daughter, Morgan

Pete with his girlfriend, Aileen

Cameron with her son, Ben

My youngest, Cameron, is 23 and has a four-year-old son named Ben. She lives nearby and we spend a lot of time together. She has worked as a customer service associate for Stanley Steemer for the past three years.

Grandchildren? I have two grandchildren, Morgan and Ben. Morgan gave birth to her daughter and decided to do an open adoption. They also named my granddaughter Morgan, and I have maintained a close relationship with her. We see her a couple times each year in California. Her parents are wonderful and very good to us. Morgan is 10.

Favorite thing about motherhood? Everything. I really enjoyed being home with them. I'm glad I earned a degree, but I've enjoyed being a mother and a grandparent more than anything else.

I was very fortunate that I was able to work from home when my kids were small. By the time I worked outside of home, my kids were in school full-time. I always made sure my work schedule was around their school schedule.

Favorite part of being a grandmother? I just feel blessed to have time with my grandson. I spend as much time as I can with him. I love doing activities such as making slime, fishing, and preparing for kindergarten. I can spoil them and be there for them.

How is being a grandparent different from being a parent? As a parent, you have a lot of decisions to make where with grandchildren, you can just enjoy them. I wish I knew then what I know now. I have great kids who have turned out well in spite of me.

What do you want your grandchildren to remember about you? I would hope they'd say that they knew they were truly loved and that I did the best I could for them. I want the best for them. Family is the most important thing.

What's the best advice you have for the next generation? Have your dreams and get the best education you can. Do something you love that you can be passionate about. Just make it happen. Don't rely on other people for things you can do for yourself, but don't be afraid to ask for help. Trust your gut and be ambitious. Grandpa never had a high school education but worked hard and at 50, lived his dream and became a millionaire. He involved and helped his entire family. Believe in God.

Biggest success? Raising my children and seeing them making their own way and being happy.

Morgan and Ben playing together on the beach

BECKY SWANSON

Becky (Swanson) and Morris Maag were married in Grand Island on December 17, 1983.

Morris & Becky Maag

1994

Where did you meet your spouse? At Kearney State College in 1982.

Courtship? We knew by the third date that we were the person for each other, and it was just unreal to us.

Engagement? He asked me at my parents' cabin and brought me yellow roses. Really we had wanted to get married earlier than we did, but my dad said, "Once you marry her, she's your problem," regarding paying for my college. So I graduated one day and got married the next day.

The Maags in 1992: Becky, Morris, Heath, and Hannah

Information about your spouse? Morris Eugene Maag: born October 10, 1960, in Lincoln, Nebraska; parents—Robert Gene and Joy Ann Schmidt Maag.

Where were you married? At the Church of God in Grand Island on December 17, 1983.

Wedding Attendants? Mark Swanson, Robert Hruska, Robert Maag, Tim Isaacs, Lori Misener, Cindy Swanson, Jeni Swanson, and Teresa Hruska.

Honeymoon? My husband had gotten a job in Ten Sleep, Wyoming, so we got married and moved the next day.

Where do you currently live?
Worland, Wyoming.

2016

Morris, Heath, Hannah, Jonas, and Becky Maag

Heath, Hannah, and Jonas Maag

Morris and Becky Maag

Where do you currently live? Chandler, Arizona

Where did you grow up? I was born in Broken Bow, Nebraska. My dad ran the Wheeler's store, then they needed him in Grand Island, so that's where I was really raised. I was maybe seven when we moved to Grand Island. He managed the distribution center. I remember liking his office. It was a glass office on the second floor so he could oversee the warehouse.

College? I graduated from Kearney State College with a teaching degree.

Career? Most of my career was teaching first grade. I taught 31 years. I really wrapped my whole life into teaching, and that was a huge passion for me. I wanted to be one from second grade on. I even married a teacher. We always had the same time off, and that made a good life for us with lots of family time.

I enjoyed everything about teaching first grade. You just see so much growth with the kids. They have such a love of learning, so much love in themselves. I enjoyed the relationships that I developed with families as well.

Morris' career? He teaches high school advanced placement mathematics. He retired but still works for the district.

Children? Hannah, our oldest, is 28 and lives in Canada with her boyfriend. She graduated from Northern Arizona University with a teaching degree but isn't teaching now. She likes doing administrative assistant work.

Heath graduated from ASU with a degree in Film and a minor in Mathematics. He works for ASU in their IT department and loves it.

Jonas lives in Gunnison, Colorado, and goes to school there at Western State Colorado University. He's majoring in Psychology and graduates in May. I'm not sure what he's going to do. He wants to go to Japan to do a teaching program there. He loves living in Colorado and enjoys outdoor activities.

Once a week we've always had a family night and get together for a meal so I hope that wherever they move, we can go see them and be happy for them.

First house? Our first place was an apartment in Ten Sleep, Wyoming. We loved it when we got up there and bought everything used because we didn't have any money. That was such a special little town—it was at the base of the Bighorn Mountains. We taught the children of these beautiful, beautiful ranch families that have been there forever. It was a K-12 school with only 80 kids. That was a great place to live and a great community to join. Eventually we moved to Worland, Wyoming, which was 30 miles away.

Hobbies? I have a book club and I love going to the movies—I see two or three a week. That's something we started when our kids were little. We tried different churches when we moved here and couldn't find one we really liked. We were both working full time and raising three kids, so Sundays were family days. We would get up and have breakfast and go to the movies. It was something cheap to do as a family.

Morris' hobbies? He's one of the Nebraska Cornhuskers' biggest fans. That's something he and Heath enjoy together, watching football and talking football. He has a good group of friends, and they enjoy having a beer together by the pool.

Are kids today different from when you first started teaching? I think the kids' developmental stages stay the same, but I know they're a lot more scheduled now. We live outside of Phoenix, and a lot of us schedule our kids. Where we started to teach, it was a ranching community and a whole different atmosphere.

Why did you move to Arizona? We had our three kids when we lived in Wyoming, and we could only see our parents once or twice a year. We wanted our kids to have a relationship with family. My parents and my aunts and uncles would winter out here in Arizona. We didn't want to be around winter that much anymore, so we decided to move. We ended up just five miles up the road from my mom and dad. Our kids got to have that relationship. It ended up being a blessing on both sides.

I miss the Midwest and like going back to see the farms and fields and farmers working. It's a really special feeling, and it smells good there. I really enjoy going home and how friendly everybody is there. They say "Hi! to everybody. I feel that both places are home.

Key to a successful marriage? A lot of laughter and doing small things for each other and doing things together. Just enjoy each other, and accept each other's strengths and weaknesses. Become one.

Favorite thing about being a mother? Just spending time with my kids. I got a kick out of every stage they went through. I enjoy seeing them develop, seeing them as adults taking care of themselves and being good to other people. Seeing them have relationships with other people is very heartwarming.

What are you most thankful for? Being born into the family I was born into. Meeting my husband and having our babies. Being able to get a teaching job that I loved so much. I really do feel very, very, very blessed.

What's the best advice you have to offer to the next generation? Keep family first, keep kids first. Do lots of stuff with family and friends. Find a passion. Be grateful every day and stay positive. Keep things simple.

Describe a perfect meal? A meal with family or friends. Maybe one made together. My favorite meal that my mom made was round steak with mashed potatoes, gravy, and green beans with bacon in them.

Biggest success? Raising kids together with my husband. Everyone who is married and has kids knows that's not easy—things don't always work out. We're both really positive people. We really have enjoyed our kids.

Biggest challenges? Just having three different kids with three different personalities and being the right type of parent for each kid. We always wanted to raise our kids to go down their own path, and we try to support that.

What do you look forward to in your retirement? I look forward to having the freedom to travel as well as the freedom of still working if I want to. I'm substituting twice a week. It's nice to be around kids—when you're around kids, you hear lots of laughter.

JENI SWANSON

Jeni, Tanner, Mike, and Tyler Akins

Mike & Jeni Akins
2016

Where do you currently live? I live in Lincoln, Nebraska.

Spouse? I am married to Mike Akins. His parents are Richard and Ann Lescinski Akins.

Courtship? Mike and I met on a blind date in Lincoln at the Old Chicago restaurant. It was a big group date. He was just really kind and funny. I knew six weeks into dating that he was the guy.

Proposal? We went to Chicago for a weekend. I didn't have an idea what he was doing.

Wedding? We got married on April 29, 2000. The wedding was a fun time. It was enjoyable getting to see my aunts and uncles dance together. It was also special for my husband because his grandparents were able to come from New York; shortly thereafter their health declined, and they passed away.

Honeymoon? We went to Disneyworld. It was fun. I had been before, but he hadn't. It was fun to do something out of the ordinary and get away.

Children? We have two boys, Tyler and Tanner. The boys are still in school.

Tyler is on the swim team and does trap shooting. He's a history buff. He must have gotten that from my dad because my dad was the same way. He is a freshman in high school this year.

Tanner plays baseball and also enjoys swimming just for fun. He is in sixth grade.

College? I went to college at the University of Nebraska at Kearney. I earned a Bachelor of Science degree in Social Work.

Career? I am primarily a homemaker. I was a social worker for 10 years or so. I worked primarily in elder care, and that job was just awesome. It was a blessing. I loved it and would love to go back, but my youngest has autism.

Mike's career? Mike was in the Army National Guard for 23 years. He retired and was hired at the VA. When veterans need benefits, they send people out to make sure the benefits are being used for the veteran. He does that and travels every couple months.

Hobbies? I love being out in my yard. I have a thing for hostas and trying to grow wildflowers. I like watching my kids play sports. I enjoy reading murder mystery suspense novels.

Mike's hobbies? He likes Star Trek.

Where did you grow up? Grand Island, Nebraska. I am the youngest out of all the Wheeler grandkids.

What was your first car? A dark green Volkswagen Rabbit convertible in high school. That wasn't supposed to be my car. They bought it for my brother Mark. He lived in California at the time. But I got the car; it was a stick shift and a load of fun. My friends called it Lurch because of the stick shift issue.

What was the best day of your life? Probably when I became a mom.

Describe a perfect meal? One with all my family around it.

Keys to a successful marriage? We've been married 16 years. To make a marriage work, you should have a really good sense of humor. We still make each other laugh. It takes a lot of work to be united as a team. I remember my mom telling me that when I was growing up – she said Grandma and Grandpa Wheeler always supported each other.

Best thing about being a mother? I enjoy watching my kids grow and shine and become the little adults they're turning out to be. They have such unique personalities.

Challenging aspect of being a mother? Raising a child with special needs.

Biggest success? The family that I have right now. They're pretty darn terrific. I'm very happy and content. I don't want for anything and am really blessed.

How has the world changed since your childhood? I don't think the world is as friendly as it used to be. There is too much media influence on people. People don't critically think about things—they just see it on the media and take its word for it. People make judgments without the facts.

What's your best advice for the next generation? Work hard, and just always have a good sense of humor about things.

INDEX

INDEX

A

Akins, Jeni (Swanson)
55, 249, 253, 275–277
Akins, Mike
249, 275–277
Akins, Tanner
249, 275, 276
Akins, Tyler
249, 275, 276

B

Basore, Amy (Wheeler)
163, 174, 176
Basore, Andy
174, 176
Basore, Gracie
174, 176
Basore, Jules Marie
176
Bloombergs, Lilly
260
Bloombergs, Stephanie (Swanson)
249, 257, 258, 259, 261
Bloombergs, Tyson
259, 261
Brookshire, Addison
241
Brookshire, Bryan
241
Brookshire, Charlotte
241
Brookshire, Chelsea (Swanson)
213, 240, 241
Bullock, Jonathan
186, 187
Bullock, Margaret Maybelle (Wackel)
163, 167, 183–186, 187

C

Chavez, Benjamin
263, 266, 267

E

Eberspacher, Shirley (Wheeler, Swanson)
35, 55, 65, 69, 77, 83, 85, 86, 89, 118, 119, 120, 213, 215–221, 224, 225, 254
Eberspacher, Stan
213, 217

F

Follstad, Eric
213, 244–247
Follstad, Hailey
213, 244, 246
Follstad, Jacob
213, 244, 246
Follstad, Sarah (Swanson)
55, 213, 243–247
Forster, Audrey (Swanson)
213, 234, 235
Forster, Brian
234, 235
Forster, Bryn
233, 234, 235, 237
Forster, Grant
234, 235

G

Gregg, Kiera
224, 227

H

Hanson, Mark
260, 261
Hof, Douglas
189, 200
Houk, Kristina
213, 240

J

Jensen, Abby
225, 227
Jensen, Amanda
225, 227
Jensen, Bruce
213, 222–229
Jensen, Cheryl
224, 227
Jensen, Connie (Swanson)
55, 118, 119, 213, 219, 222–229
Jensen, Kyle
213, 223–228
Jensen, Lilli
225, 227
Jensen, Lucas
225, 227
Jensen, Stuart
213, 223–228

L

Long, Morgan
265, 267

M

Maag, Becky (Swanson)
55, 119, 249, 253, 268–274
Maag, Hannah
249, 269, 270, 272
Maag, Heath
249, 269, 270, 272

INDEX

Maag, Jonas
249, 270, 272
Maag, Morris
249, 253, 268–274
Misener, Cameron
266
Misener, David
249, 253, 262–267
Misener, Lori (Swanson)
55, 119, 249, 253, 262–267
Misener, Morgan
249, 253, 264, 265
Misener, Peter
249, 264, 265
Murphy, Wayne
79, 81, 82

P

Pac, Alyssa (Panning)
189, 193, 202–205
Pac, Lincoln
203, 204
Pac, Ulysses
203
Palmer, Darwin
189, 193, 199
Panning, John
189, 193, 202–205
Panning, Pamela (Wheeler)
55, 189, 202–205
Panning, Rachael
189, 193, 202–205

S

Swanson, Adam
213, 240
Swanson, Bailee
213, 240, 241
Swanson, Beverly (Wheeler)
55, 65, 69, 77, 83, 86, 89, 118, 119, 220, 249, 251–256
Swanson, Bob (Robert)
55, 86, 118, 119, 120, 130, 213, 215–216
Swanson, Brett
213, 232, 233, 235
Swanson, Carly Anne
213, 232, 235
Swanson, Cassidy Nicole
213, 232, 235
Swanson, Cindy (Mettenbrink)
249, 253, 257–261
Swanson, Desiree
249, 253, 257, 258, 261
Swanson, Mark
55, 118, 119, 249, 253, 257–261
Swanson, Megan
213, 240
Swanson, Mike
55, 118, 119, 213, 219, 224, 238–242
Swanson, Peter
55, 118, 119, 130, 249, 253
Swanson, Stephanie
213, 238–242
Swanson, Steve
55, 118, 119, 213, 219, 224, 230–237
Swanson, Terri (Sekeres)
213, 230–237

T

Tuma, Jim
130, 145, 189, 193, 194–197
Tuma, Mary Kay (Wheeler)
55, 118, 119, 189, 193, 194–197
Tuma, Sarah
189, 193, 195, 196, 198

W

Wackel, Debbie (Wheeler)
55, 110, 119, 163, 168, 179, 182–188
Wackel, Nicholas
163, 183–186, 186
Wackel, Tim
163, 179, 182–188
Wheeler, Bill
55, 119, 189, 193, 206–212
Wheeler, Buzz (Bruce)
55, 86, 130, 163, 168, 172–178, 179
Wheeler, Byron
55, 118, 119, 163, 179–181
Wheeler, Carol
189, 206–212
Wheeler, Eric
163, 172, 173, 176
Wheeler, James Louis
209
Wheeler, Jim
55, 72, 81, 86, 89, 92, 110, 118, 119, 129, 189, 191–193
Wheeler, Katherine
189, 208, 209
Wheeler, Lloyd
55, 65, 85, 86, 118, 119, 129, 165–171
Wheeler, Margaret (Grandma Wheeler)
5, 35, 41, 48, 55, 59–159
Wheeler, Maybelle (Lundgren)
55, 86, 165–171
Wheeler, Mona (Murphy)
55, 81, 86, 89, 118, 119, 189, 191–193
Wheeler, Patti (Wackel)
163, 179
Wheeler, Sheila
172–178
Wheeler, Sue
55, 118, 119, 189, 193, 199–201
Wheeler, Ted (Lloyd Wheeler, Grandpa Ted)
2, 3, 40, 55, 59–159

www.ingramcontent.com/pod-product-compliance
Lightning Source LLC
Chambersburg PA
CBHW060502240426

43661CB00006B/890